Listening to Children's Wishes and Feelings

A TRAINING PROGRAMME

Mary Corrigan and Joan Moore

BAAF
ADOPTION
& FOSTERING

British Association for Adoption & Fostering
(BAAF)
Saffron House
6–10 Kirby Street
London EC1N 8TS
www.baaf.org.uk

Charity registration 275689 (England and Wales) and SC039337 (Scotland)

© Mary Corrigan and Joan Moore, 2011

British Library Cataloguing in Publication Data
A catalogue record for this book is available from the British Library

ISBN 978 1 907585 16 6

Project management by Shaila Shah, Director of Publications, BAAF
Designed and typeset by Helen Joubert Design
Printed in Great Britain by The Lavenham Press

BAAF is the leading UK-wide membership organisation for all those concerned with adoption, fostering and child care issues.

To Peter and our four children, for their generous love and support over the years of my freelance career and all the children and parents I have had the pleasure to work with.

Mary Corrigan

To Graham and our two children for all their love and encouragement, and to the children and parents in foster and adoptive families with whom I have had the pleasure to work.

Joan Moore

Contents

Contents

About the authors

Mary Corrigan has a background in nursing and social work. At present, she works as an Independent Social Worker, Child Care Consultant, Play Therapist and Trainer for several London boroughs and voluntary agencies. Since 1975, she has specialised in working with children and families in transition, helping them to understand what is happening to them and supporting them to form new attachments when their placement becomes permanent.

Mary teaches the attachment–trauma–loss interface, the development of self and the direct work/life story sequence on the Post Graduate Diploma in Advanced Social Work, Children and Families MA at Kingston University, and similarly at Royal Holloway University, Bedford Square and Brunel University. She wrote an earlier version of her *Listening to Children* course in 1990 and teaches this to many London boroughs, voluntary adoption agencies and Children's Guardians for NAGALRO and CAFCASS. She supervises play therapists and runs direct work skills supervision groups for social workers. She has also written articles and presented papers on direct work with children.

Joan Moore is a Dramatherapist, Play Therapist, and an Adoption Support Agency, with a background in social work. Currently, she provides therapy to children and families in adoptive and foster care, expert witness assessments, supervision for creative arts therapists, and teaching on direct work for local authorities and related agencies.

Joan's "Theatre of Attachment" model involves adoptive parents and foster carers in performing their children's life history, often in fictional contexts. It developed from her research into child development, attachment, loss and trauma, which examined a variety of perspectives for the purpose of helping children to reattach safely.

Joan has written *Stories and Drama for Children in Care: A creative approach for adoptive and foster families* (working title) due to be published by BAAF in 2012; *Creative Problem Solving: Therapeutic story and drama for schools and families*, due to be published by Hinton House in 2012; a chapter in Jennings S. (ed) (2009) *Dramatherapy and Social Theatre*, published by Routledge, and articles, including 'Theatre of Attachment' in *Adoption and Fostering*, 2006.

Acknowledgements

As practitioners, we are aware that, like the group who wrote the original training pack, we have leant on the shoulders of many thoughtful and creative teachers and families. Most of all, we have learned from the children involved. Our thanks go to all those parents and children with whom our work has been incorporated in the form of pictures, stories and vignettes. We have taken care to protect their confidentiality and also ensure that our work is culturally sensitive. We hope to inspire you all to bring listening to your work via the direct/ non-directive use of stories and metaphor.

We also thank all those at BAAF for their help in putting this pack together and Carol Schaessens for her editorial input.

Our special thanks go to Margaret Adcock and Dr David Hodgson at Kingston University; also Lisa Gordon Clark, Carole Samuels, Lynda White, Jay Vaughan, Pene Sinnot, Diane Hanlon, Fiona Peacock, Fran Taylor, Linda Hoggan, Jo Williams and Imran Rumjon, all of whom have given helpful suggestions and encouraging feedback in their peer reviewing of our work through its various stages. Our warm thanks also to the social workers, adoptive parents and foster carers who asked for the advice that prompted this work, particularly those who have read sections of it and reported the benefits with such welcome enthusiasm.

On a personal note . . .

Many other colleagues and friends have also given me valuable support and advice.

I would especially like to thank Professor Sue Jennings, and to pay tribute to the late Phillip Maddock, who demonstrated such impressive commitment in expanding therapeutic services for children in the care of Northamptonshire.

Joan Moore

I would like to add a special thank you to my supervisors, who have taught me so much over the years, and without whom I could never have taught or played with children with so much enjoyment. They include: Dolly Lush, Margaret Adcock, Jane Maltby and Jenny Kendrick, and my personal therapist, Dayle Thackray. I hold you all in the highest regard.

Mary Corrigan

Foreword

When BAAF published the original *In Touch with Children* course in 1984 there was a great deal of enthusiasm and demand for assistance in developing more practitioners' skills in working with children. Nessie Bailey, the BAAF Northwest consultant, had already encouraged many agencies to develop very good services and had introduced UK social workers and carers to Vera Fahlberg and the importance of attachment theory. Some wonderful work was done by social workers with children and families, portrayed, for example, in *Working with Children in Need: Studies in complexity and challenge* edited by Eric Sainsbury (Jessica Kingsley Publishers, 1994).

Sadly, within a few years after this levels of knowledge and skills seemed to be dwindling away. Many social service departments were restricting the time practitioners in children and families teams could spend with children. Agencies providing adoptive families often only had responsibility for supporting the carers and not the children. Even students on post-qualifying courses had difficulty finding a child with whom they could undertake direct work

Not surprisingly there is now a good deal of criticism and both public and governmental concern about the failure of social workers in relation to children. There is again a demand for better, more skilled work and this requires the provision of good quality training.

I cannot think of anyone better suited to initiate a revival of skilled direct work with children than Mary Corrigan and her co-author Joan Moore. Mary's skills in developing and presenting techniques for working with children and inspiring new practitioners are legendary, as so many former students would testify. Joan's work on the handbook will help practitioners to incorporate new theory and knowledge at the same time. I am delighted to recommend this new training course from BAAF. Its publication is timely and its content is excellent. I hope that *Listening to Children's Wishes and Feelings* will be very widely used.

Margaret Adcock
October 2011

Preface

The *Listening to Children's Wishes and Feelings* course and handbook were inspired by and have their roots in the *In Touch with Children* course, published by BAAF in 1984. The original course was devised by Nessy Bayley and Daphne Batty, who wrote and collated work given them by a group of committed and creative individuals who worked eclectically with children, using the symbolic language of play. They collaborated in order to write a training manual and course to help social workers to listen to children. In the acknowledgements, they state:

This can truly be described as a corporate exercise. Who knows, for instance, who was the originator of the pat-a-cake game that is an important step in the development of a small child?

We feel the same. Everything included in this course and book is the result of trial and error – by others or by us – with the children and families with whom we have worked. In 1984, Mary was working for Westminster Social Services with Cynthia Flood. Developing methods from the original course, they created a framework and guide for social workers doing direct work and so it was that the *Listening to Children's Wishes and Feelings* course was born.

Since then, thanks to painstaking research and practice by others in this field, Mary has been able to update and add material culminating in the creation of this new course and handbook in collaboration with Joan Moore.

Having each worked with many adoptive and foster families over the years, we realised that children need to "walk" their story in order to reattach safely, while their parents depend on help to understand and resolve their children's problems. This requires us to explain complex theory and, alongside much needed emotional support, to provide an ever-expanding set of creative skills, tools and stories. We both work in the child's home where we find that children, feeling safer, will transfer the magic of learning taking place in the "play space" to everyday life in the same setting.

This training programme and accompanying Handbook are the outcome of our work with families and all the involved professionals who support them. We draw from many strands of theory, in particular, developments in neuroscience over the past 15 years, which have contributed enormously to our understanding of child development, attachment, trauma and loss. We aim to integrate these strands in order to make them accessible and expand practitioners' and parents' confidence to use their own creativity with children. Mary Corrigan developed the training programme and guidance on assessing and supporting children through loss and transition, while Joan Moore worked mainly on the handbook, in particular, collating the theory and the chapters on play, dramatic approaches to life history and therapeutic stories. A comprehensive range of techniques with guidance is supplied on the CD that accompanies the Handbook.

Mary Corrigan and Joan Moore
September 2011

Introduction

The need for this training programme

All social workers and parents need to be able to help children share their wishes, feelings and worries. The problem is that if you ask a child a question they will often answer by saying what they *think* you want to hear. However, by using direct work techniques, it is possible to learn how to communicate in the child's language at times when they are scared and traumatised.

The purpose of this course is to help participants develop the ability to listen to children more effectively, so that their real needs, wishes and feelings can be heard. This is a four-session experiential course, which aims to teach participants the theory that is the foundation for good practice in communicating with vulnerable children. This theory underpins all the exercises, which are further explained in the *Handbook* and *Techniques CD,* both essential reading for trainers running this course and for the participants they are training.

It is our hope that course participants will gain confidence in using both listening and play skills, and in this way find that the theory and skills gradually become integrated within their practice.

Who is this course for?

The course is intended as training for the following groups:

- all social workers – the course can be included in social work MA programmes and post-qualifying social work courses, as well as being used as part of induction training for social workers;
- family support workers in assessment centres and residential care workers;
- foster carers and adoptive parents, and some kinship carers.

What we hope this course will achieve

The course will enable participants to:

- better understand how a child's attachment and development of self is affected by loss, trauma and/or a disrupted childhood;
- learn about ways in which children communicate their wishes and feelings through their behaviour and play, and identify where risk may be present in a child's family situation;
- help children deal with loss, express their emotional needs and manage strong feelings;
- use reflective listening skills and assessment techniques with children to identify their needs, wishes and feelings, in the context of the *Framework for the Assessment of Children in Need and their Families* (Department of Health, 2000);
- work with children to process difficult past experiences so as to develop a sense of identity (in the context of their particular culture, ethnicity, religion and gender);
- assist children in processing and recording their life history so they can repair, build resilience and have hope for their future;

- support children as they prepare to move to a new home, attach to new parents or reattach to birth parents, and maintain links with other family members when separation from them is the agreed plan or outcome;
- support parents in helping children express needs and use self-calming strategies;
- know when it is necessary to seek professional help and supervision in order to look after oneself while carrying out this demanding and complex work.

Course overview

The course is a four-day or four-session programme, with one follow-up session, and it can be delivered as a whole or in modular form. (For more details on how to run it, see 'How the course can be delivered' in the section 'How to use this training programme'.)

There is an accompanying *Course Handbook* – referred to as the *Handbook* – and *Techniques CD* (at the back of the *Handbook*) and both are essential reading for you as the trainer and for course participants. These enhance the material in this course and give advice and techniques you can use to back up the material in the programme. For this reason we strongly advise that you, as trainer, familiarise yourself with this book as doing so will remind you of what you already know, as well as enhancing your presentation points and making it easier to find the techniques you need as you go through the course. The CD also contains the PowerPoint presentations, accompanied by trainer's notes, as well as the handouts.

It is important to advise participants in advance of the course that it is advisable that they get hold of a copy of the *Handbook* and look through it prior to attending the course.

The material of the course is divided up and delivered as follows:

Sessions 1 and 2

- Session 1: **Attachment and trauma:** Child development; the interface between attachment, trauma and loss; essential listening skills.
- Session 2: **Managing difficult feelings:** Working within a "framework for direct work"; grief; assessment, and ascertaining a child's wishes and feelings; managing complex behaviours.

Sessions 3 and 4

- Session 3: **Building a positive self-esteem and starting a life history journey:** Transition work; promoting self-esteem, positive identity and resilience; commencement of life history work.
- Session 4: **Moving and re-attachment:** Moving children without trauma; attachment in new families; endings; how to look after yourself emotionally when doing this work.

Session 5

This should be undertaken within six months of completing the block of four sessions described above.

- Session 5: **Revision day:** Groups to review any play techniques they have used with children in their own cases; discussion of managing contact; looking at how to tell difficult stories to adopted children; special guardianship/kinship care; reunification.

The programme can usually be fitted into a day that runs between 9.30am and finishes at 4.30pm. We have suggested the likely length of the various sections into which the day is divided. However, as the course is run in a workshop style (i.e. allowing discussion), the times of the day at which each specific part starts will vary. We have therefore not indicated specific times for each section.

Make sure you plan how you will run the morning and afternoon so as to fit in all the material to be covered. Clearly, the time allowed for group tasks and feedback will also depend on your group size. However, it will also depend on participants coming back from breaks and lunch promptly and this should be pointed out to them in the Welcome session.

How to use this training programme

What trainers need to know

If you are the person who will run this programme (i.e. act as the trainer of the participants on this course) it is essential that you:

- have skills in direct work with children;
- are familiar with adult learning principles;
- are committed to anti-discriminatory practice;
- are familiar with the course content and are confident in delivering this.

See also 'Using more than one trainer' below.

How many participants should attend the course

We suggest that the number of participants should be no fewer than 8 and no more than 20.

How the course can be delivered

We have found that the most effective way to teach this course is to:

- Deliver Sessions 1 and 2 consecutively.
- Then give the participants a week off (to catch up on their work).
- Then deliver Sessions 3 and 4.
- Deliver Session 5 as a follow-up session within six months of the participants undertaking the original course.

(*Note*: When setting dates be aware of the need to avoid half-term or religious/festive holidays.)

Another option would be to deliver the course a day at a time over four weeks.

If you are an experienced trainer, you may feel able to mix and match some of the modules to create your own course, and this is acceptable providing you cover the theory of attachment, trauma and loss and the principles and practice of communicating effectively with children. However, it is generally better to immerse participants in the whole course so that the theory and techniques become integrated into practice.

Finally, the course can be used to create a shorter, one-day course called 'Ascertaining children's wishes and feelings' for social workers or Children's Guardians. This could be done by combining relevant material from both Session 1 and Session 2.

Using more than one trainer

As mentioned above, it is essential that this course is delivered by a trainer who has experience of direct work. However, often courses like this are run with two trainers – one who has a good knowledge of the theory and the other who has had practice in direct work and thus has an understanding of children's responses to the work.

If you are a trainer who has little practical experience in using direct work, you will need to deliver the course with a co-trainer who has the necessary skills and with whom you can practise the techniques before demonstrating them on the course.

What this pack includes

In addition to this *Trainers' Guide*, this training course requires you to have all the following items:

- the **Course Handbook** (as mentioned above), which is a guide that should be read by both the trainer and the participants. You will need to have a copy of this and familiarise yourself with it, as well as ensuring that all participants have access to it before and during the course;
- a **Techniques Guide**, which is on the CD at the back of the *Handbook*. This describes what is needed for, and how to carry out, the activities and exercises that you will be demonstrating to participants during the course – these are individually numbered and particular activities are referred to by number in this guide. This will need to be printed out and photocopied so that there is a copy for every participant on the course, and should be given out at the beginning of Session 1;
- a **CD** with all the **PowerPoint presentations** used in the course along with notes, **case studies** and a set of **handouts**, which you will also need to print/photocopy and give out to participants on relevant days. This CD is at the back of this *Trainer's Guide*. (There is a list at the beginning of each session detailing which handouts and case studies you will need to have with you on that day.)

Resources and equipment you will need

Below is a list of all the equipment you will need throughout the entire course. Specific resources needed for particular sessions are listed within the session.

General equipment and resources needed for running the course

- A flipchart with plenty of paper (as many exercises need this) and plenty of coloured felt-tip pens
- A laptop computer with CD-ROM drive and PowerPoint software
- An A4 pack of plain white paper
- A projector and screen for displaying the PowerPoint presentation (usually supplied by venues but you should check this)
- A DVD player and TV screen
- Printouts of all the handouts for participants, which can be found on the CD at the back of this *Trainers' Guide*, and which include the course and session overviews
- Printouts of the PowerPoint slides to give to participants
- Enough copies of the *Handbook* and *Techniques CD* to hand out to participants in Session 1
- Evaluation forms and/or certificates for course participants from your department or agency
- A list of participants to tick off on registration
- Refreshments for when participants arrive and for coffee and tea breaks
- Name badges and folders for participants to put handouts in
- A list of the dates on which later modules of the course will take place

● Copies of books that will be of use to participants during and after the course (see further details below).

Extra things needed for specific exercises during the course

You will need the following. (Advice about how to obtain some of these items is given below and on the *Techniques CD*. It may also be possible to find some of the toys required for the course at an education resource centre, or from a local assessment centre.)

● Pens, pencils, coloured felt-tip pens for the participants and some means of pinning up what they draw on flipchart sheets (e.g. Blu-tack).
● Enough paper plates for each participant to have one and a small amount of play sand in a lightweight container: enough for a small handful for each plate. (This equipment is used to provide small sand trays for a listening exercise in Session 1.)
● Small multicultural dolls and wild or domesticated animal toys, for use in the sand trays in an ecomaps exercise at the end of Session 1. You will need enough of these for the number of participants on the course. You will need at least five cars, dolls and animals so that each participant has a family group of more than four objects. Having a box of buttons is an alternative, or you can ask participants to bring their own small toys – in which case you will only need in addition a couple of toy families (e.g. Playmobil ones as well as a car and some animals).
● A bag containing sensory and feelings equipment. (For more details about this bag and its contents see the list of play equipment and materials in the *Techniques CD*.)
● A puppet (preferably an animal one) for demonstrating listening skills using a third object with young children, and a couple of old mobile phones or telephones.
● A doll that is big enough to cradle in your arms, for an optional exercise in Session 1.
● Paint: finger or poster paint with 20 brushes. (This is for the four seasons exercise in Session 3.) If you do not want to use paint for any reason, then felt-tip pens can be used. However, paint better stimulates sensory memories, thus enabling children to access feelings and talk about them.
● You may also find a small drum useful for demonstrating certain techniques.
● You will also need the equipment necessary to demonstrate the water game and the candle ceremony in Sessions 3 and 4. (See the *Techniques CD* for a list of the relevant equipment.)
● Other items that will be useful for demonstrating exercises on the course include:
    – at least 20 balloons
    – some silly putty
    – a small pile of magnets
    – a few pots of bubbles
    – some pots of coloured slime (which can be obtained from Hawkins Bazaar online).
● It would be helpful to have copies of the following books (full details of which can be found in the book list at the back of the *Handbook*):
    – *The Little Prince* by Antoine Saint-Exupéry for the end of Session 1
    – *Muddles, Puddles and Sunshine* and *Managing Difficult Behaviour* for Session 2
    – *Draw on your Emotions* for Session 2
    – Examples of life story books for adopted children and life story work for Session 3. (See the back of the *Handbook* and www.baaf.org.uk/bookshop for more details about these.)
    – *Dennis Duckling* and *Chester and Daisy Move On* for Session 4.

DVD material that can enhance learning

This material is optional but well worth having if at all possible.

- For Session 1: A training DVD, *Attachment for Foster Care and Adoption*, Part 1, by Mary Beek and Gillian Schofield, published by BAAF (see www.baaf.org.uk/bookshop for details). This DVD is particularly helpful because it shows mothers really connecting to their babies and gives a demonstration of the "Strange Situation" procedure, which is useful in assessing the attachment style of a parent and child.
- For Session 4 or 5: A DVD, *Jannie's Story on Trauma and Re-Enactment*, which shows how children bring behaviour from their past parenting experience into their new placement. This costs £100 and can be obtained from Family Futures (see www.familyfutures.org.uk). (Whether you decide to use this will depend on the specific work your participant group is engaged in, i.e. whether they are adoptive parents or foster or kinship carers.)

Preparing for the course

When you send out information about the course to participants, ask them to bring a puppet or soft toy, which can be used in different activities throughout the course.

As mentioned earlier, during the course you will be doing an "ecomap" exercise, for which you will need small toys for use by the whole group. If you think you won't be able to get hold of enough small toys yourself, we suggest you ask participants to bring one group of the following small toys with them, such as:

- a Playmobil multicultural family group;
- some small plastic animals, both domesticated and wild species;
- a small box of mixed buttons or fake jewels;
- some organic objects, like shells, bark, stones, etc.

It is possible for you to collect these together gradually yourself or purchase them at small cost from a website (see in *Techniques CD* under *Play equipment and materials*). However, asking participants to get hold of these will encourage them to start a small collection for their own future use. But since some participants may forget to bring these, we advise that you do bring some along yourself!

It is important that participants familiarise themselves with the *Course Handbook*, so it is advisable that they are given copies before the course begins.

Diversity issues

It is your responsibility to ensure that the course is accessible to everyone and that all participants – whatever their ethnic background, sexuality or educational level – feel equally valued, respected and heard for the life experiences they bring. As a trainer, you need to be sensitive to the composition of the group and consider how you will include and address the needs of participants who are from minority ethnic groups, who have a disability, who are single or who are gay or lesbian.

You should make sure all the dolls and books you use reflect a multicultural society and that any text used is in no way discriminatory. As mentioned above, when setting dates be aware of the need to avoid half-term or religious holidays.

It is useful to try to find out in advance about any participants with special needs in order to plan how to include them in the exercises and to ensure that the venue is suitable for their needs (see below). Asking participants in advance will forewarn you, for example, about the need to have a British Sign Language interpreter or the need to provide handouts in a larger type size. (The handouts are provided as Word files, and therefore the point size can be altered.)

For people with acute visual impairment it can be helpful to send copies of any notes to be used on the course well in advance, and in an accessible format, so that they can read these on their own computer.

The venue

When choosing a venue you will need to find one that accommodates at least 20 people.

The room must be big enough to accommodate the group if it needs to be split into four groups of five. There should also be enough space to have tables for groups of five or six participants to sit around, that are large enough for them easily to be able to look at their copies of both the *Handbook* and *Techniques CD* printouts when necessary.

Many exercises are carried out in pairs so there should also be room for people to move into pairs.

Arrange enough chairs for participants in a horseshoe shape, with a table at the top for your equipment. Put the toys to be used in the course at the front of your table.

Make sure you consider the needs of those with disabilities and then check the following kinds of issues with the venue organiser:

- that a parking space will be available for participants with mobility difficulties, close to the building;
- that the building/toilets/training room are accessible;
- that the lights are not flickering;
- that there are facilities for participants with a hearing impairment – they may, for example, need a hearing loop, or have a particular need to see your face clearly when you are communicating with them.

Running a training group

Creating a safe environment for learning

Clearly, this course deals with some extremely sensitive areas of human experience – feelings related to attachment, separation, trauma and loss. Both you and all the participants are likely to have experienced for yourselves the emotions around such experiences to a certain extent. However, some participants may not have allowed themselves to revisit these losses and emotions for some time, and could therefore find these particularly upsetting.

As this course is necessarily experiential and will be thought provoking for all involved, it may well cause some participants to need to speak to the trainer privately and you should make a point of mentioning and then reminding participants about this possibility each day in the welcome session.

Participants should be advised that if they start to feel overwhelmed, or strongly affected by a particular issue, they should sit out of an exercise, or, if they wish, merely observe. If it becomes necessary, they should be permitted to discontinue the course and perhaps seek confidential support professionally. (This rarely happens, and participants should be made aware that this outcome should not affect their jobs.)

In addition to dealing with any emotions that the course throws up, participants should be made aware at the outset of the course that they will need to show utmost respect, sensitivity and complete confidentiality in dealing with other course participants, and with any information shared during the course. Ground rules should be set and participants will need to be reminded of these.

Managing group dynamics

As a trainer, you may find that managing group dynamics is complex, especially as this course is designed for multidisciplinary groups. The types of groups that have to be considered on this course are:

- the group as a whole, i.e. all participants, and
- smaller groups that people will be divided up into in order to carry out tasks.

What often happens in groups is that some people will want to dominate while others then don't get a chance, or feel unable, to speak. If this problem arises, remind participants that each individual needs to have a chance to express themselves and all participants should respect and listen to each other's contribution.

As a trainer, you also need to be aware of the emotional temperature of the group and be prepared to change an exercise if you feel it is necessary. You may find that using the driving game, balloon fights game or clay work can help you achieve this without your having to be directive.

In the large group situation, when someone asks a question to which you don't know the answer, you may find that asking whether someone else in the group knows the answer, or has an opinion on the matter, can facilitate open and productive discussion. And you can also agree to find out the answer in time for the next session.

Useful reading

Before running this course you may find it useful to refer to the following books:

- Armstrong H, Britton B and Pickles T (1991) *Development Training Skills*, New York: Longman Group Ltd
- Howarth J and Morrison T (1999) *Effective Staff Training in Social Care: From theory to practice*, Basingstoke: Routledge & Young Ltd

The website www.eureka-tp.com is also a useful resource for designing and facilitating training sessions.

SESSION 1
Attachment and trauma

OVERVIEW

	Section	Timing
1	Welcome	**10 minutes**
2	Setting ground rules	
3	Starter exercise: *Getting to know each other*	**10 minutes**
4	Setting the scene for the day: *Course aims and goals for Session 1*	**20 minutes**
5	Exercise: *Identifying children's needs*	**30 minutes**
6	Presentation: *The development of attachment and a core sense of self* (includes showing DVD or doing an exercise if DVD not used)	**50 minutes**
7	Break	**15 minutes**
8	Feedback on DVD (if shown)	**10 minutes**
9	Continuation of presentation on attachment	**10 minutes**
10	Exercise: *Using a third object*	**15 minutes**
11	Looking at loss	**25 minutes**
12	Lunch	**1 hour**
13	Exercise: *Introducing oneself to a child*	**30 minutes**
14	Presentation on trauma	**25 minutes**
15	Break	**15 minutes**
16	Listening to children	**30 minutes**
17	Exercise: *Listening through play*	**20 minutes**
18	Closing the session	**10 minutes**

PREPARATION

In preparation for delivering and adding to the presentations below, read the following chapters in the *Handbook* so you understand fully the PowerPoint slides and are able to elaborate on the points made:

- Chapter 1: *Child development*
- Chapter 2: *Attachment*
- Chapter 3: *Neglect*
- Chapter 4: *Grief and loss*
- Chapter 5: *Play*

PARTICULAR RESOURCES NEEDED FOR THIS SESSION

The following is a summary of the particular materials needed for today, over and above the list on p. 5:

- PowerPoint presentation Session 1
- Refreshments to offer on arrival and for tea and coffee breaks
- Lists of participants to tick off on their arrival
- Name badges and folders to put handouts in
- Enough copies of the *Handbook* and printouts of the *Techniques CD* for all participants
- Some spare copies of the *Handbook* and *Techniques CD* in case participants forget to bring them
- Information on health and safety
- Examples of books that participants will find helpful in doing this work, such as those mentioned at the end of the *Techniques CD*. Particularly helpful are books for children that explain complex subjects in metaphor
- A doll large enough to cradle in one's arms
- A feelings bag (for instructions on this see the *Techniques CD*)
- A glove puppet
- Bubbles
- Silly putty
- A variety of puppets and a set of old telephones
- A few mixed packs of fuzzy felt. (These are to show participants what they might use in their work. When you show them, suggest that participants read instructions in the *Techniques CD* about using these.)
- Groups of toys or animals
- A pile of magnets
- Zen garden (No. 42 on the *Techniques CD*)
- "What do you feel?" cards
- Emotional learning cards
- Enough paper plates for each participant and a small amount of play sand to go on them
- A copy of *The Little Prince* (this is optional)

HANDOUTS

- 1.1: *Session 1: Overview*
- 1.2: Information notice explaining health and safety and lunch arrangements (you will need to draw this up yourself)
- 1.3: *Eco-map*
- 1.4: Toy bag for participants to draw in.
- 1.5: The six-stage model of bereavement and the effects of secondary trauma
- 1.6: Diagrams of brain from the left and right, with Notes
- 1.7: *Running a direct work session*
- 1.8: *Listening skills*
- Copies for each participant of Session 1's PowerPoint presentation slides

10 minutes   **1   WELCOME**

Before participants arrive, display Slide 1, which shows the title of the course. This should stay up until Slide 2 is shown.

SLIDE 1
Listening to children's wishes and feelings

As participants arrive, ask them to tick their name off a list you have prepared. This will then enable attendance certificates to be produced for those who have attended all four sessions.

Also offer participants refreshments on arrival.

Once the group has fully assembled, go through the following points.

- Introduce yourself, giving a short resumé of your career.
- Acknowledge that participants have given up valuable time to attend the course and point out that there is a lot to cover.
- Distribute Handout 1.1 – Session 1: Overview.
- Explain health and safety issues and where fire exits and toilets are – distribute Handout 1.2.
- If necessary, remind participants that this is a two-day module of a four-session course. Tell them the dates for all the days, including the date for the potential follow-up day.
- Point out where you have put examples of books to look at that they will find useful after doing this course.
- Give out name badges to be filled in and folders in which they can put handouts throughout the course.
- Finally, ask participants to please turn off their mobile phones/Blackberries.

2   SETTING GROUND RULES

- Set out clear ground rules such as being on time starting, finishing and after breaks. Tell participants when breaks are scheduled and ask them to take care to respect boundaries about time, as this will ensure that all the tasks can be completed.
- Explain that this course requires that everyone practises utmost confidentiality regarding client names or anything private that may come up for participants during the course.
- Say that as this course is necessarily experiential and will be thought provoking for all involved, it may well cause some participants to need to speak to the trainer privately if they are finding something difficult emotionally. Let them know when you would be available for this.
- Say to participants that they should also monitor how they are feeling about material presented and that if they start to feel overwhelmed, or strongly affected by a particular issue, they can choose to sit out of an exercise.

10 minutes   **3   STARTER EXERCISE: GETTING TO KNOW EACH OTHER**

Ask participants to get into pairs and introduce themselves, telling each other their names and explaining their specific involvement with children. Then get participants back into a main group and ask each pair to introduce the other person to the group and briefly say what they do.

It is helpful if you make notes as the participants go around the group, as this is your chance to be aware of particular skills or interests in the group.

20 minutes

4   SETTING THE SCENE FOR THE DAY: COURSE AIMS AND GOALS FOR SESSION 1

Explain that Session 1 will be a mix of theory and experiential exercises and so participants should expect to spend much of it listening to some presentations. However, they will be doing a few exercises in pairs, or in small groups, with the aim of becoming familiar with certain tools that can be used in working with children.

Explain that the purpose of doing these exercises is:

- so that participants experience for themselves the potentially very powerful emotional effects of a particular exercise on a child, in particular, using a "third object" (such as a puppet or toy) to facilitate communication;
- to help participants get in touch with their own feelings during direct work, in order that they can understand how it feels for a child.

Tell participants that this is not a therapeutic course but it necessarily brings up issues in our own backgrounds while looking at the backgrounds of children we are working with. Remind them that they only have to share what they are comfortable about sharing. Explain that when talking in the main group, you will only ask about techniques, not any personal information they share. If for any reason anyone wants to sit out of an exercise, let them know that they can – no explanation will be required.

Go on to explain the aims of the course in general and this particular session, using Slide 2 Aims of the course and Slide 3 Goals for Session 1.

 SLIDE 2
Aims of the course

- To expand and apply knowledge of child development
- To understand the theories related to attachment, trauma and loss and the emotionally stuck child
- To develop a framework within which to work creatively and communicate with children
- To get in touch with the child in us, so that we can be playful and use techniques for working with children
- To plan how to do this work in your workplace or home

 SLIDE 3
Goals for Session 1

- To study the needs of a growing child and the building of "self"
- To understand the theories of attachment, trauma and loss
- To learn how to listen to children through a third object

After showing Slide 3, explain that these slides have shown the areas of theory that participants will need to understand before they can move on to ideas about listening effectively to children.

Show them Slide 4, The strands of growth, which lists the basics of child development, and explain the information using the Notes that accompany the slide.

SLIDE 4
The strands of growth

Physical	Emotional
Sensory	Social
Intellectual	Moral

30 minutes   **5**   ## EXERCISE: IDENTIFYING CHILDREN'S NEEDS

- Ask participants to get into groups of about five people, i.e. four groups if you have 20 participants.
- Show them Slide 5.
- Ask the groups to discuss and list what they think are the needs of children from birth to adolescence, using the headings on the slide (as this makes it easier for feedback comparison), and completing what is missing below the final heading ('As children grow older they also need...').
- Give out flipchart paper and pens to each group.
- Suggest they nominate someone to feed back for each group.
- Tell groups that they have 15 minutes to complete this exercise.

SLIDE 5
The needs of children

- Basic needs
- Psychological needs
- As children grow older they also need...

FEEDBACK ON EXERCISE

Ask groups to feed back from their discussions in the last exercise. Put up their flipchart answers on walls, if possible. The answers should cover the following points, and if any are omitted then go through these with participants once all feedback has been taken.

Basic needs

- Food, clean water, shelter, clothes
- Warmth, sunlight and fresh air
- Space to move and play
- Protection from illness and injury
- Training in self-care and safety

Psychological needs

- Holding, carrying, rocking and cuddling
- Affection, companionship and conversation
- Continuity of individual care (it's better for the child if they don't have multiple carers to model from, although, in some cultures, child care is shared within the extended family)
- Familiar environment with routines but also new experiences
- A sense of identity and self-worth
- Self-respect, from receiving praise and encouragement
- Self-control, from learning to regulate emotions

As the child grows older they also need...

- Opportunities to learn from experience and to make mistakes
- To increase independence in personal, social and financial matters
- Opportunities to take responsibility for their behaviour and beliefs
- A sense of thoughtfulness for others
- Opportunities to make helpful contributions at home or in a social group

These needs relate to the outcomes in *Every Child Matters* (DfES, 2003).

Explain that if these needs are not met, the child's overall physical and mental health could be impaired or delayed and the child may not feel, or be, safe.

Say that you will next be going on to explore how children attach and how the attachment process supports the development of a core sense of self.

50 minutes

6   PRESENTATION

The development of attachment and a core sense of self

In order to have a basis for our work we need to carry out a comprehensive assessment of a child's:

- developmental delay (if any);
- attachment style;
- trauma and grief state;
- wishes and feelings.

The exercises and material in the course are designed to help participants make such an assessment.

If you are going to be using the DVD during this presentation, then just show Slides 6, 7 and 8 and then introduce the DVD.

If you are *not* going to show the DVD then after Slides 6–8 you should continue with Slides 9 and 10 (see instructions below).

As you go through the slides, use the Notes that accompany them.

SLIDE 6
The self

The child in you:	I want
The parent in you:	I should
The adult in you:	I think
Three "captains" in you:	Who's in charge?
The ego state:	The self

(Idea from *Gestalt theory*, Woldt and Toman, 2005)

Explain that you will be talking more about the idea of "identity" in Session 3, but the ideas in Slide 6 show the Gestalt view of self. If any participants aren't familiar with Gestalt as an idea, then explain briefly as below.

Gestalt therapy was a form of psychotherapy created by Fritz Perls, a German-born psychiatrist, and his wife. The core idea of the Gestalt therapy process is developing in the user an enhanced awareness of his or her sensations, perceptions, bodily feelings, emotions and behaviour in the "present moment". Relationship is emphasised between the self, its environment and the other.

Elaborate on Slide 6, referring to the Notes on the PowerPoint presentation.

Slide 7 introduces the idea that from birth we evolve a series of different "selves". Show Slide 7 and explain it using the information below.

SLIDE 7
The self

- 0–2 months ⟶ Emerging self
- 2/3–7/9 months ⟶ Core self
- 9–18 months ⟶ Subjective self
- 2 years ⟶ Verbal self
- Beyond ⟶ Narrative self

(Stern, 1985)

In order for a baby to form a secure attachment and to develop a sense of self, he or she needs a responsive parent whose mind is focused on the baby/child. This is called "attunement" (and is seen when mothers and their children mirror each other's facial expression and mood). If you are going to be showing the DVD, say that participants will see this illustrated in the DVD that follows later.

Explain that children develop their sense of self by going through a number of quick stages, which you can describe using the Notes.

Bonding and attachment

Say that in Slide 8 we look at the ideas of "bonding" and attachment.

Although many of your participants may be familiar with these terms, it's probably worth reading out the following information about attachment before showing Slide 8.

- 'In attachment theory, the word "attachment" has a specific meaning. It is a tie based on the need for safety, security and protection. This need is paramount in infancy and childhood when the developing individual is immature and vulnerable.' (Prior and Glaser, 2006)
- The parent *bonds* to the child, which means that the parent/carer makes a relationship with the child by meeting his needs and attuning to the child. The child *attaches* to the parent as he gets his needs met by the parent.
- The core concept of attachment theory is that a dependent infant needs a loving, protective care-giver who bonds to the child by understanding her feelings and managing her feelings on her behalf (i.e. by responding to them) and by being "mind minded" (a term that is used in the DVD). Parents build this bond by starting off a "conversation" with the child and then taking it in turns with the baby to have the conversation. Even though the baby only appears to be babbling, the parent responds by chatting and smiling back at the baby's efforts to communicate.
- If the parent is able to do this, then the baby's feelings won't overwhelm him, he feels secure enough to explore the world and they can enjoy it together.

SLIDE 8
Bonding and attachment

Parents bond to child...
...child attaches to parent

Showing the DVD

If you are using the DVD, then at this point play Part 1 of the DVD *Attachment for Foster Care and Adoption* by Mary Beek and Gillian Schofield – 'Core concepts in attachment theory'. This will take you up to the break. Ask participants to make a note of the attachment behaviours they observe.

If you *don't* have a copy of the DVD, then show Slides 9, 10 and 11, supplementing these with information from Chapter 2: *Attachment* in the *Handbook*. You can break up your lecture on these slides by doing one or more of the exercises described after Slide 11 below.

Attachment cycles

Discuss Slide 9 as follows.

The next two slides come from Vera Fahlberg's work, published in 1994, and help us look at attachment in more detail.

- "Attachment" does in fact refer to something that we use all the time in forming relationships. We first learn "attunement" and how to regulate our emotions via our parent's careful reading of our needs and feelings.
- Our parents are usually able to "attune" to our needs and feelings because of their *own* experience of attachment, i.e. when they were babies and their own parents were responsive to their needs and so they had their needs met. This means that when a parent's own baby cries they can recall the parenting they received themselves and can respond when the child shows a need, because they can identify with the child's needs.
- This promotes a bond of attachment between parent and child.

SLIDE 9

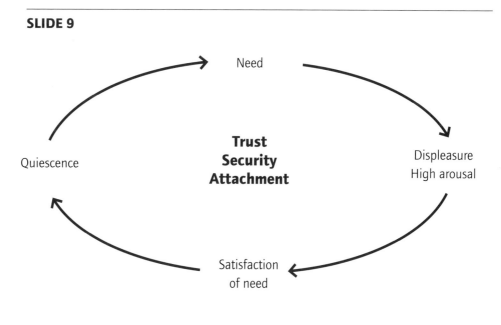

(Fahlberg, 1994)

Show Slide 10 and draw attention to the direction in which the arrows go, pointing out how self-esteem is enhanced by positive parenting. Where the direction is reversed in this cycle then the children are having to parent the parent. In this case, they usually have a low sense of self-worth, although they present as very controlling and confident.

SLIDE 10

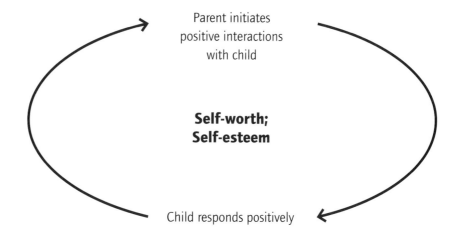

(Fahlberg, 1994)

What are attachments?

Explain that in Slide 11 you will see some further points about this, which are explained in Chapter 2: *Attachment* in the *Handbook*, to which you can refer participants.

SLIDE 11
What are attachments?

- Close emotional tie or bond
- Haven of safety
- Protection through helping child regulate feelings and behaviour
- Attachments are only one part of the parent–child relationship
- Attachments to other family members lead to a "hierarchy of attachments"

Exercises on attachment for trainers without the DVD

Demonstrating attunement

This method can help bypass the child's "stuck self" via sensory stimulation.

Hold the doll you have brought with you for this day's course and use this to model attunement. Ask participants to watch how, in your role here of parent/carer, you examine the baby closely using all your senses, i.e. voice, fingers, eyes and gaze, taste and kisses, and blowing on to skin, holding close and rocking. Show how you give the baby absolute attention, and in this way "claim" the baby. When you have done this, then go into the following demonstration, which is useful when wanting to engage shut-down children. (This exercise will not be appropriate for children who have experienced physical or sexual abuse.)

It is a good idea to have practised this with a co-trainer before demonstrating it to participants.

- Choose a participant nearby (use someone who doesn't seem timid or shy) and ask for their permission to take their hands in yours.
- Explain that to get the full attention of a young child (aged below eight years) it is a useful technique to ask the child if they could give you their hands. (It is usually the carer who will be using this method so there is already a modicum of trust.) Take their hands in yours.
- Do this to the participant and gently stroke the backs of their hands with your thumbs upwards towards their wrists, saying each of the following:
  - 'Can I see your eyes?'
  - 'You really wanted me to know that you could do that' (using a *praising* tone) or
  - 'That is something you may not do' (something you'd say if they were, e.g. throwing a stone – this means "no" in a gentle way).

Ask the participant to tell the group what they felt during the exercise.

Ask if he or she noticed the sudden eye contact that being stroked gave him or her. It is usually impossible to avoid this eye contact. This technique mimics a mother stroking an infant's cheek upwards while saying soothing words.

Then explain that even the most shut-down child will hear a message if she is receiving the positive early attachment behaviours her mother should have used.

If you still have additional time after the last exercise, try this next one.

Differing attachment styles

Tell participants that this extra exercise is intended to show participants how it feels to be with a child who has what is called an "ambivalent attachment style" or who has an "avoidant attachment style". (Say that these different styles of attachment will be explained later.)

Knowing how it makes one feel to be with anxiously attached children will be useful when doing an assessment and thinking about how to place this child, e.g. how might this child make a carer feel?

- Get participants, in pairs, to try out introducing themselves to someone.
- Ask one person in each pair to behave like an anxious child, e.g. fidgeting in their chair with their eyes wandering all over the place.
- Ask them to spend two minutes on this.
- Then ask participants for feedback on how it made them feel. (It probably made them feel anxious or frustrated.)

Then:

- Ask the pairs to swap over.
- Get the other participant to behave in an avoidant manner, e.g. staring angrily at the person or studiously avoiding all eye contact.
- After two minutes, ask how it felt to speak to somebody who was behaving like this. (It probably made them feel frustrated, then angry and maybe a little hurt.)

15 minutes   **7**   **BREAK**

10 minutes   **8**   **FEEDBACK ON DVD IF SHOWN (SEE BELOW IF NOT SHOWN)**

Ask the group what they enjoyed most about the DVD and what they noticed about the parent–child interaction. Write down their answers on flipchart paper. (They will probably pick on points about attunement through the senses and reciprocity.)

Once you have gone through this feedback, then continue at (9) below with the presentation on attachment using Slides 12–18.

If you did not show the DVD, continue immediately with the presentation on attachment using Slides 12–18.

10 minutes   **9**   **CONTINUATION OF PRESENTATION ON ATTACHMENT**

Now present Slide 12, which explains more about attachment theory.

SLIDE 12
Principles of attachment theory

- Children are born with the disposition to become attached to their care-givers.
- Children organise their behaviour and thinking to maintain these attachments, which are key to their physical and psychological survival.
- Children often maintain such relationships at great cost to their own functioning.
- Distortions in feeling and thinking that stem from early attachment disturbance occur most often in response to parents' inability to meet the child's needs for comfort, security, affect and behaviour regulation, and emotional reassurance.

(Marvin, 2002)

Now show Slide 13 and explain that this is from Bowlby's (1973) work on attachment. John Bowlby was the first person to describe attachment theory and, with the help of Mary Ainsworth and Mary Main, four types of attachment were identified, as we will see shortly.

Briefly give a case example of a child displaying these behaviours if you have one from your caseload.

SLIDE 13
Reaction to disruption in attachment

The protest–despair–detachment cycle
- Protest – crying, distress, pursuit of mother, searching after the mother, temper tantrums
- Despair – depression, quiet withdrawal, refusal to be comforted by the stranger, disinterest in play or exploration
- Detachment – lack of interaction with the primary care-giver after reunion, active avoidance of the care-giver, and failure to recognise the care-giver

(Bowlby, 1973)

Interface between attachment, loss and trauma

Explain that you will now be thinking about the interface between attachment, loss and trauma. To do this we need to look at the effects on attachment of the neglect and trauma that is so common for the children we work with.

Explain that in Slides 14 and 15 you will first be presenting some ideas about the different attachment styles from research by John Bowlby (1983), Mary Ainsworth (1979) and Mary Main (1989–90).

Use the information given in the Notes to supplement your explanations of the content of the slide.

(If you require further explanation of the material in Slides 14 and 15, refer to Chapter 2: *Attachment* (pp 20–21) and Chapter 3: *Neglect and trauma* in the *Handbook*.)

SLIDE 14
Types of attachment

Group A: Secure attachment
- Child is comfortable, calm in the parent's presence
- Child is wary, anxious when the parent departs
- Parent is consistently responsive
- Reciprocity in the interaction between parent and child
- Child is secure and seeks help

Group B: Insecure–avoidant
- Child displays a high level of motor activity
- Child is unperturbed when the parent leaves
- Child is non-reactive when the parent returns
- Parent is insensitive and inhibited
- Parent avoids bodily contact
- Child sees the parent as likely to rebuff

SLIDE 15
Types of attachment (cont)

Group C: Insecure–anxious/ambivalent
- Child is fearful, agitated when parent leaves
- Child will not be soothed when parent returns
- Parent is insensitive, minimally responsive and gives delayed, inconsistent, inappropriate responses
- Child sees the parent as not available or responsive
- Parent is enmeshed

Group D: Disorganised
- Child's behaviour is bizarre, extreme
- Child overtly rejects, punishes and disciplines the parent
- Child humiliates the parent
- Child provides caretaking to the parent
- Parent is ineffective, inconsistent and helpless and child can be frightening to the carer
- Child sees the parent as useless, punitive

Show Slide 16 and then explain how critical situations affect "secondary attachment", i.e. an attachment that is not to your biological parent, kinship or foster carer. For example, illness requires dependency, so during a period of illness a child might reach out for a new carer and thus what appears to be an attachment is formed, but it may be a "kinship through trauma", and the carer does not really feel to the child like a secure base. ("Kinship through trauma" can be defined as being a bond created between two people going through a life-threatening experience together. However, such a bond is not one of love but one related to surviving this frightening experience; it is also sometimes called a "trauma bond".)

In these situations the child remains very insecure and does not gain positive self-esteem as a result of the placement because they are always expecting to be moved on, as they haven't been through the proper attachment process with the new carer. Their feelings are stuck and the child does not go through the grieving process for the loss of their primary care-giver.

Unless they can be assisted to go through this grieving process, the child will not move on emotionally.

SLIDE 16
Critical situations that elicit attachment behaviours

- Illness
- Unavailability of care-giver
- Presence of stranger
- Aloneness
- Darkness
- Novel settings
- Injury
- Danger
- Hunger
- Fatigue

(Bowlby, 1973)

Show Slide 17 and explain how babies do things in order to establish and maintain attachment. Remind participants that they will have noticed some of these behaviours in the DVD (if shown).

SLIDE 17
Infant/child attachment behaviour

- Eye contact
- Smiling
- Pouting
- Protesting separation
- Following
- Searching
- Reaching
- Signalling or calling to
- Holding or clinging
- Seeking to be picked up
- Sitting with

Show Slide 18 and explain that in the work we do with children our aim is to build a good sense of self, as described in the "integrated self" we see on the left-hand side of the slide. Children who have been subjected to trauma or neglect show signs of a "fragmented self", as described on the right-hand side of the slide.

Then go through the accompanying Notes, which deal with this in more detail.

SLIDE 18
Building of self

Safety	*Threat*
● Integrated self	● Fragmented self
● Resonating affect	● Reactive affect
● Flexible behaviour	● Impulsive behaviour
● Reflective thought	● Rigid thought
● Coherent narrative	● Disorganised narrative
● Presence	● Dissociation

(Hughes, 2000)

Explain that children who have been traumatised and who have fragmented selves find it hard to feel reciprocal enjoyment such as fun and love whilst learning to make relationships. They often show minimal empathy and the carers who live with these complex children may feel manipulated by them – failing to understand that the child is living in a state of abject fear and shame and is often hyper-aroused. Children like this may be unable to tolerate intimacy and this gives carers little immediate satisfaction from caring for the child. The carer's tolerance thus often runs out and they become harsh with the child and can be autocratic.

15 minutes   **10**   ### EXERCISE: USING A THIRD OBJECT

Show Slide 19. Explain that if children can be assisted to get in touch with their senses they can then begin to find words for their feelings.

SLIDE 19
The senses

Explore the five senses

Give words for feelings

Say that you will now be doing an exercise to show how the use of a third object can help a child get in touch with their feelings. Remind participants of the "emotional health warning" you gave earlier.

For this exercise you will need to have a "feeling/sensory bag", in which you have collected a number of small toys, play figures and objects like shells, as well as sensory-stimulating objects like a lavender bag, TCP or a smelly lotion, a rubber, wooden toys or bits of cloth with different textures. (See other suggestions listed in the equipment and materials section in the *Techniques CD*.)

● Pass the sensory/feelings bag around the group and ask each participant to take an object out of it.
● Tell participants to close their eyes and to smell, touch and feel their object, and to then consider what it reminds them of. Explain they have a couple of minutes to do this.

- Then ask participants to describe their sensory experience of the object and any memories it evokes. (Participants are likely to come up with childhood memories from the touch, sound or smell of a favourite childhood toy.)
- When you have finished gathering participants' feedback, ask them what they noticed when listening to each other describing their memories.

Explain that emotional and sensory experiences are encoded in our limbic system and mid-brain, below the cerebral cortex, which is the thinking part of the brain (which participants will be learning about later on). This means that when the senses are stimulated by these objects or toys, we can gain access to our emotional and sensory memory, which is unconscious.

Explain that children's choice of toy or object in an assessment is often unconscious, especially if they have unresolved traumatic memories. Their choices may be informed by their unconscious sensory memory, and this can have significance when we are trying to listen and notice what they are playing or saying.

Children can communicate with us through a third object (perhaps a toy), which can let us know how they feel about themselves or about an occasion they suddenly remember – which may pop into their brain like a lightbulb being switched on, thereby enabling them to see the experience very clearly again. Ask participants to reflect on this – have they observed children doing this?

Explain that you will be looking again at this later in the afternoon, as well as in later parts of this course.

25 minutes   **11   LOOKING AT LOSS**

Note: As the trainer, you should have read Chapter 4: *Grief and loss* in the *Handbook* prior to going through these next two slides.

Also, be aware that we deal only briefly with loss in Session 1 and that Session 2 has been designed to go through the full presentation. This is because when participants do the first exercise in Session 2, it may put them in touch with their own losses but they will have time to process these during other exercises in the morning of Session 2 (e.g. "Managing difficult feelings") and during the rest of that day.

Say that you will now show Slides 20 and 21:

- Slide 20 illustrates the stages in the process of loss.
- Slide 21 shows diagrammatically how this is manifest in various grieving stages experienced by the child, and how these, in turn, cause secondary trauma in the carers/parents. (Point out to participants that Slide 21 will also have relevance when we look at making a good assessment, in the next session.)

SLIDE 20
Loss and separation

First stage: Isolation, shock, numbing
Second stage: Underestimation, yearning and pining
Third stage: Depression, denial, disbelief and anger (bargaining)
Fourth stage: Despair then testing
Fifth stage: Discovery, acceptance
Sixth stage: Revitalisation, hope

(Elisabeth Kubler-Ross *et al*, 1969)

Loss is an extremely important part of many children's experience, and any loss generates a grieving process. Say that you will look at the various stages of this process in detail in Session 2, explaining how to manage each stage and practising the techniques that go with it. Explain that the reason we are looking briefly now at loss is so that participants can learn about the effect of loss on attachment and to help them understand why they need to learn about brain damage this afternoon.

Tell participants that when they are going to do an assessment they will need to know the significance of the interface between attachment, trauma and loss. It is important that participants understand what *stage* of loss a child is at. This is because the child may simply be stuck in trauma or at a particular stage of the loss cycle, rather than having some big underlying problem relating to attachment, as is often mistakenly supposed.

Show Slide 21 and then go through the Notes – distribute Handout 1.5, which contains all this information. (There is also more detail about this in Chapter 4: *Grief and loss* in the *Handbook*.)

SLIDE 21
The six-stage model of bereavement and the effects of secondary trauma

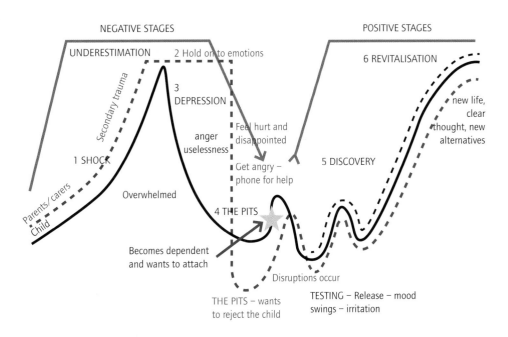

The six-stage model of bereavement and the effects of secondary trauma

Explain to participants that they can use this diagram to show clients where they or their child might be in terms of stages in their loss. It can be very helpful for clients to see that the diagram charts a road to recovery.

Explain that the dark line on the diagram is the child's grief and the dotted line is the resultant secondary trauma on the child's parents/community. Then explain the slide, using the Notes, and relating these explanations to the numbering of each line above.

Say to participants that you will be looking in more detail at the ideas on this slide when we look at making a good assessment, in the next session.

The inner working model

Before showing Slides 22–24, explain the meaning of the term "inner working model" as described by Bowlby (1969): 'By 36 months the partnership between child and parent has solidified'; and Delaney (1991): 'an optimistic expectation, mental representation or blueprint regarding himself'.

Show Slide 22 and explain that when a child has a *negative* inner working model, as demonstrated in their conduct, the carer starts unconsciously to re-enact it under the emotional pressure (which then reinforces the child's model).

SLIDE 22

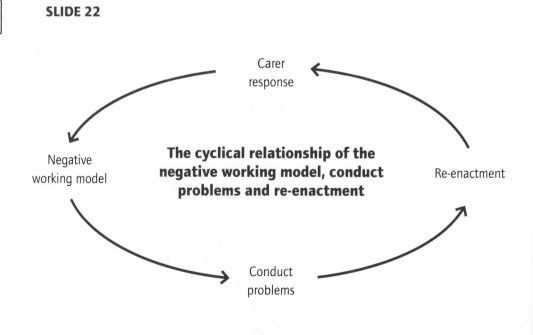

Show Slides 23 and 24, using the additional explanation given in the Notes.

SLIDE 23
Carer reaction or countertransference

- Feelings of impotence
- Urge to reject the child
- Abusive impulses towards the child
- Emotional withdrawal and depression
- Feeling like the bad parent
- Sexual feelings for the child

(Delaney, 1991)

SLIDE 24
Child re-enactment

- Recreates old relationships with new people
- Gives meaning to disjointed conduct problems
- Signals an underlying negative working model
- Presents barriers to attachment formation
- May result in sabotage to the carer home placement

(Delaney, 1991)

After showing Slides 23 and 24, explain that after lunch you will be looking at how trauma affects a child's brain.

Point out that there is a list of attachment games in the section titled *Child Development and Attachment* on the *Techniques CD*. Participants may at some stage be able to help clients to try these games if they have attachment-resistant children. These games, which are based on "thera-play" ideas, are really important in encouraging appropriate attachment styles in new placements. It is also a good idea for social workers to give their clients a list of these.

1 hour	**12**	**LUNCH**

30 minutes	**13**	**EXERCISE: INTRODUCING ONESELF TO A CHILD**

- Start by asking participants to get into groups and to spend 15 minutes discussing the following questions, which you should have written up on the flipchart.
  - How do you introduce yourself to a child you are to work with?
  - What might you use to help you with this?
- Then get participants to feed back for 15 minutes.

When you have heard feedback from participants, do the following:

- Start by reminding everyone that most of our communication as humans is conveyed via our body language and tone of voice so, clearly, that is important to consider when you introduce yourself to a child.
- Then demonstrate some introduction techniques that might be helpful. There are several ideas about how to engage children on the *Techniques CD*.

Hand out the picture of the toy bag (Handout 1.4), and suggest that participants start filling this in with a list of toys they would like to put in their personal toy kit from this point in the course. This will act as a reminder of the kinds of things they might use to help them work with a child.

Useful ideas for toys to engage children include the following:

- different types of bubbles to engage young children;
- silly putty to engage a child, who can make an animal with it – this stuff also bounces and is fun for children to play with;
- puppets or telephones to give distance to pain via a metaphor;
- pictures using fuzzy felts to explore sibling group relationships and experiences in the same family;
- groups of toys, animals or people for house play.

To engage adolescents you can use:

- silly putty because they can fiddle with it (thus soothing them as they talk to you);
- a pile of magnets to fiddle with;
- Zen gardens instead of sand tray eco-maps using organic matter or objects. Zen gardens are a sort of miniature sandbox for adults. Sand boxes are useful because in them one can create a visual map of the family and community around the child. We look more at this in an exercise after the break;
- "What do you feel?" cards and "emotional learning cards";
- pens and paper to draw with. Mention the value of Margot Sunderland's books *Draw on your Emotions*, and *Draw on your Relationships*. (See the book list in the *Handbook*.)

Having demonstrated how to use some of the above ideas, say that you will go on to look at "rules of engagement" in sessions with children, and at interview boundaries after the break.

25 minutes **14   PRESENTATION ON TRAUMA**

The sources for the following presentation are as follows:

- lectures given by Vera Fahlberg from 1982 to 1998
- a lecture by Bruce Perry in 1997
- Danya Glaser in Prior, Vivien and Glaser (2006) *Understanding Attachment Disorders: Theory, evidence and practice*
- *Why Love Matters* by Sue Gerhardt (2004)

You will find it helpful if you reread Chapter 3: *Neglect and trauma* in the *Handbook* before presenting this.

Explain that now that participants have had a bit of activity by doing an exercise, you will be finishing the essential theory before moving on to do some direct work. This next set of slides looks at how neglect and trauma affect a child's developing brain.

Show Slides 25a and Slide 25b, which describe the development of the brain, and then go through them using the Notes. The diagrams and Notes are also available to distribute – Handout 1.6.

SLIDE 25A
Brain viewed from the left

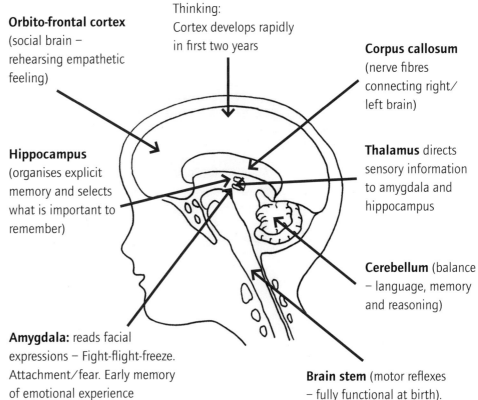

Orbito-frontal cortex
(social brain –
rehearsing empathetic
feeling)

Thinking:
Cortex develops rapidly
in first two years

Corpus callosum
(nerve fibres
connecting right/
left brain)

Hippocampus
(organises explicit
memory and selects
what is important to
remember)

Thalamus directs
sensory information
to amygdala and
hippocampus

Cerebellum (balance
– language, memory
and reasoning)

Amygdala: reads facial
expressions – Fight-flight-freeze.
Attachment/fear. Early memory
of emotional experience

Brain stem (motor reflexes
– fully functional at birth).
Controls heart, lungs, muscles,
blood pressure and temperature

Early life trauma is encoded at a
motor sensory level
Two responses to fear:
1. Rapid survival decisions – amygdala
2. Slow cortical – context and inhibition –
    orbito-frontal cortex and Hippocampus

SLIDE 25B
Cross-section of the brain

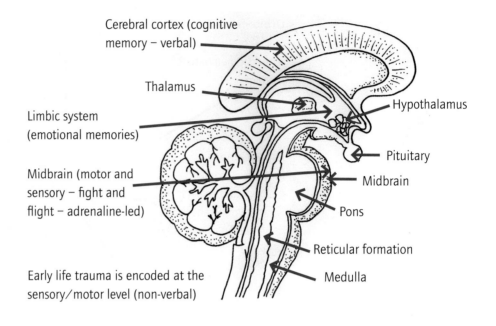

Cerebral cortex (cognitive memory – verbal)

Thalamus

Limbic system (emotional memories)

Midbrain (motor and sensory – fight and flight – adrenaline-led)

Early life trauma is encoded at the sensory/motor level (non-verbal)

Hypothalamus

Pituitary

Midbrain

Pons

Reticular formation

Medulla

Now introduce Slides 26–29, which elaborate further on brain development and brain damage. As you go through them, add the additional information given. (If you need to understand this more fully, you can refer to Chapter 3 in the *Handbook* for more detailed explanations about how the brain functions.)

SLIDE 26
Brain damage

● The endocrine and neuro-hormonal products of arousal associated with severe or prolonged stress can affect the infant's brain development.
● High levels of cortisol produced by a traumatic event cause atrophy in the frontal lobe.
● Nutritional deficiencies and any toxic substances consumed by the mother may cause brain damage in the unborn child.

SLIDE 27
The brain nerve cell

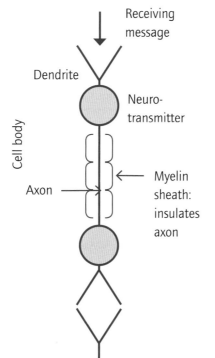

Receiving
message

Dendrite

Neuro-
transmitter

Cell body

Axon

Myelin
sheath:
insulates
axon

Early brain development
- The nerve cells of the brain grow on a 'use or lose' basis.
- 83% of the brain develops after birth.
- 0–3yrs sets the attachment template.
- The brain is 90% of its adult size by 4yrs.
- The brain's plasticity makes it highly receptive, dependent on care to thrive, and is easily damaged.

Trauma
- As a result of stress the brain cell is damaged.
- The myelin sheath insulates the axon like plastic does to a copper wire.
- Cortisol, the waste product of adrenalin, damages the sheath and the electrical impulses can no longer be passed to the dendrites.
- On scans, black holes can be seen where this damage occurs.

SLIDE 28
The frontal lobe of the brain

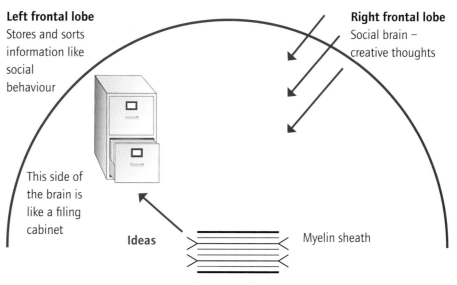

Left frontal lobe
Stores and sorts
information like
social
behaviour

Right frontal lobe
Social brain –
creative thoughts

This side of
the brain is
like a filing
cabinet

Ideas

Myelin sheath

Corpus callosum

If the brain cells are damaged in this part,
it is not always possible to retrieve the
information. So children in stress often have
poor short-term memory

SLIDE 29
Brain development

- Sensory stimulation influences neural growth.
- Neglect causes atrophy at the developmental stage when it occurred.
- Perry and Pollard (1997) – For optimal brain development the child needs consistency, predictability and nurture.
- Early regulation of babies' emotions has a major impact on the organisation of the brain.

After going through Slides 26–29, explain about early life, referring to the Notes.

Show Slide 30 and then use the Notes to explain it.

SLIDE 30
Physical effects of acute stress

The areas of the brain that are involved in the acute stress response also mediate:
- Motor behaviour
- Affect regulation
- Anxiety
- Arousal
- Sleep
- Cardiovascular and respiratory function

The relationship between trauma and attachment

Introduce Slides 31–33 and then amplify Slide 33 using the Notes.

SLIDE 31
Most children:

- have many opportunities to experience manageable amounts of frustration and pain
- learn how to contain (manage) affect and cope with pain
- develop a strong sense of self

(Briere, 1992)

SLIDE 32
Traumatised children:

- do not learn affect modulation or how to contain their pain
- those who have been abused will experience affect modulation in three ways:
    - interference with development of attachment and trust for others
    - decreased self-awareness because of hyper-vigilance
    - less exploration of the world
- have a poorer sense of self

(Briere, 1992)

SLIDE 33
Healthy attachments

A healthy attachment helps counteract the effects of trauma
- The child has learned a basic sense of trust.
- The child has learned self-soothing skills, which work for him or her.
- The child looks to trusted care-givers for comfort post-trauma.

Explain the implications of the above.

- Therapeutic approaches must take into account the persistent fear state that traumatised children experience and must be directed at the areas of the brain that mediate this alarm–fear–terror continuum. To alter these memories, one must be in the state that regulates that part of the brain, via the senses (Perry and Pollard, 1998).
- Cognitive and verbal interventions won't affect this part of the brain. You will need to use sensory stimulation to soothe and calm the child.
- The major way to affect the primitive parts of the brain is to provide predictability, nurturance and support – to help the child feel safe, comfortable and loved.

The Four Fs

Explain that Slide 34 shows an easy way to remember what children need: "the four Fs". If these four ideas are used by carers who are re-parenting traumatised children, these children will eventually become less reactive. Once you have shown Slide 34, go through the Notes.

SLIDE 34
The Four Fs

What children need most of all is the following:
- Familiar...routines, regular warm patterns to the day; food; sleep; hugs
- Fun...A sense of humour, free play to explore and use imagination
- Firm...clear boundaries with empathy
- Friendly...to be heard with emotional warmth, have hugs and belong.

(Corrigan and Floud, 1990)

The less anxious a child is, the more likely any interventions will be successful: when a traumatised child becomes dysregulated, they are often in a state of terror and display the behaviours of fight, flight or freeze. We will discuss these in detail in the next session when we look at managing difficult behaviour.

Very early memories (including trauma) are encoded on a sensory-motor level and affect self-regulation and identity. Useful interventions with traumatised children can therefore include the following:

- sensory-motor integration therapies, such as hand massage (see the *Handbook* Chapter 1: *Child development*, Chapter 2: *Attachment* and Chapter 5: *Play and communication*, for details of these);
- action-type therapies, such as drama, music and play;
- sensory integration: cooking, claywork, drama and movement, etc.;
- music: the rhythm of certain music can be helpful in accessing feeling states;
- smells: these can stimulate memories;

● naming, categorising and classifying objects.

Resolving childhood issues

Explain that, according to Van der Kolk *et al* (1996):

'People have to remember, to heal...If they don't remember they don't know why their body keeps playing tricks on them' (meaning they continue to see and feel things that others are not experiencing).

Mary Main (1990) identifies five necessary steps in the resolution of any childhood issues:

1. Face the pain.

2. Acknowledge the ongoing influence of one's early life.

3. Arrive at an understanding of why care-givers behaved as they did.

4. Identify what the individual wants to repeat and not repeat.

5. Muster resources for support of change.

15 minutes	**15**	**BREAK**

30 minutes	**16**	**LISTENING TO CHILDREN**

It will be helpful if you remind yourself of the contents of Chapter 5: *Play and communication* in the *Handbook* (where you will find material summing up the purpose of play) before running this part of the session.

Explain to participants that in this section you will be taking them through material that covers the following.

● Why we need to listen to children and how to do so
● Ideas about transference and countertransference
● Dan Hughes's "PACE", which is a quick way of remembering what we need to demonstrate with children in terms of how we behave with them in a session
● How to run a session
● Points to remember when doing assessment for court work
● Ways of listening empathetically
● How to prompt a child to expand on what they're saying
● The importance of reflecting feelings

Introduce Slide 35 and use the Notes to explain it. (Mention that you will shortly go on to look at transference and countertransference, in case anyone is unsure what this means.)

SLIDE 35
Listening to children

- To listen, we have to make a deliberate effort to recall and use our own experience of childhood, if we are to reach the child.
- We have to understand how to listen to our own feelings so we can understand the child's (transference and countertransference).
- We need to separate children's behaviour from their feelings, and to do this we have to concentrate on their basic needs.

Transference and countertransference

Explain that when listening to children in their play it is really important to try to be aware of how we are feeling when we are with that child. This is because part of what you feel will be the result of you picking up on what the child is feeling (what is known as "transference"). What they feel (and what you then feel) will tell you something about how the child has experienced previous relationships of an intimate nature. When parents and professionals are aware of how they are affected by their child (transference), they can also see how their reaction to this (countertransference) can impact on the child. There is a clear explanation of these two terms in Chapter 5: *Play and communication* (p. 61) in the *Handbook*.

The importance of being aware of what you are feeling is that it will guide you to appreciate how the child feels. You will find more on this in Chapter 5: *Play and communication* and Chapter 6: *Assessing children's needs, wishes and feelings* in the *Handbook*.

Explain that parents can learn to understand the feelings that are aroused in them by their children's behaviour, as follows:

- When a child needs ATTENTION in perhaps an irritating way, you may feel ANNOYED.
  If at that point you can take time to think about how you are feeling, you will probably become aware that the child's behaviour is about needing attention. Once you are aware of this, you can try doing any of the following: play with them, or do something soothing using sensory materials (e.g. using warm water, bubbles or warm play dough; give older children or young people some faux fur to stroke or a soft toy); do some clay play or cooking (making pizza or cakes, for example, enables them to share the produce and receive affirmation from those they share this with).
- When the child enters a POWER contest, you may feel ANGRY.
  In these circumstances, set boundaries and try to stay in your own space. (We will learn more about this in Session 2.)
- When the child seeks REVENGE, you may feel VERY HURT.
  It's important then to remember that the child is seeking revenge for the past, usually not against you. Stay in a safe place yourself but don't move out of sight. Allow the child some "angry space" and acknowledge hurt without making it into something good or bad: we feel as we feel. Afterwards, show affection and bonding to the child with a cuddle, soothing language and encouragement.
- When the child shows INADEQUACY, you may feel HOPELESS/HELPLESS.
  Go back to the child's previous developmental stage and nurture the child to show reassurance and encouragement. With the child, review a past achievement, move or change so that the same strategies already achieved can be used to overcome the present inadequacy. For example, if you ask the child to lay the table but they refuse to, give them a puzzle or

something that is below the capabilities of someone of their chronological age. When they complete it, praise them for remembering how to do it and then suggest they put it away and lay the table. This reminds the child of their competency.

● When the child seeks APPROVAL of FRIENDS, etc. you may feel WORRIED/ANXIOUS.
The child again needs reassurance and approval for the simplest things that they are achieving daily, so, using reflective listening, play the counters game (see Game No. 23 in Techniques CD) to encourage the child's self-esteem and your empathy with his/her worries.

(Corrigan and Floud, 1990)

Explain that you will now go on to briefly talk some more about listening skills, and then go through general advice on setting up and running a session with a child, in which you will give some practical examples of how to use listening skills (see also Chapter 5: *Play and communication* in the *Handbook*).

Listening skills

Explain that in any session with a child you must establish sufficient trust for the child to see you as a non-threatening, reflective listener who makes them feel safe. You can do this by using paraphrasing and listening skills. Tell participants that there are many ways to practise good listening, some of which are described in the *Handbook* in Chapter 5: *Play and communication*, and Chapter 6: *Assessing needs, wishes and feelings*, and in the drawings – see the *Techniques CD*.

Also helpful are:

● Axline's model (1967): Axline was influenced by Carl Rogers' person-centred counselling (1961), which has eight principles of practice (see Chapter 5: *Play and communication* in the *Handbook*). She starts with a free play session, in which it is important to set boundaries, as described below;

● the work of Rise Van Fleet (1994, 2011), who has written several books and training courses on the filial play method, the origins of which are in the work of the Drs Guerney, in which parents run play sessions with their children so as to help attachment and develop their problem-solving skills. In order to be child-centred in your session, it's important to practise Dan Hughes's idea of PACE, as described below in Slide 36.

PACE

Say that, in every hour you are with a child, you need to use PACE, which stands for the ideas given in Slide 36.

SLIDE 36
PACE

P – playfulness
A – acceptance
C – curiosity
E – empathy
Equals LOVE

(Hughes, 2000)

In order to ascertain how children see their world, we must:

- help them express their wishes and feelings;
- notice developmental delays;
- use transference and countertransference, as described above.

Running a direct work session

Go through the following ideas with participants, based on the work of Van Fleet with Topham (1994, 2011). (Participants will find this reproduced in Handout 1.7.)

- *Starting and setting boundaries*: Lay out the toys or things you have with you. Explain 'the toys stay on the mat/in the room', and say 'You can do almost anything on the mat. If there's something you may not do, I'll let you know.'
  If the child tests the boundaries by, for example, throwing something at you, you would say something like:

  I said I would let you know if there is something you may not do, and that is something you may not do but you can do almost anything else. (If you just say "no", the child may freeze or become controlling.)

  If the child persists in doing something dangerous, warn them again and if they then don't stop, tell them the session has ended for today but you will come back for the next session. Then close the toy box or remove them from the room.

- *Life history*: If you are doing life history work, or working with a child for more than just three sessions, the child will need a memory box, a small chest of drawers or folder. Carers or parents could be asked to provide them with a plastic chest of drawers (such as can be bought from a DIY store) with three or four drawers, in which they can store their memorabilia, pictures, stories, birthday cards, life story books, and larger models made at school.
- *Regularity of sessions:* Do keep to the date and times of sessions as the child will become anxious if you let them down, and then won't trust you.
- *Ending the session:* Always warn the child five minutes before the end of the session that the session is coming to an end. Give them a sticker at the end or read a story that reflects the play session, giving the child a choice of books for you to read a story from if you can.
- *Number of sessions:* Tell the child clearly how many sessions there will be and name each session clearly as you go – letting the child know when the last one comes with plenty of warning and having prepared a little goodbye. As it can be hard for social workers to make time for this work, be aware that life journey work sessions can be accomplished in blocks of six sessions at a time. However, be honest with the child about the number of sessions you can provide and don't make promises you can't keep about how often you will see them.
- *Ending a block of sessions:* When you are coming to the end of a block of sessions, give the child plenty of time to realise that you are parting for good. Tell them at least three sessions in advance as this will allow them to feel angry and control part of the goodbyes. (Remember, life has never let them have this choice before.)

Assessment and court work

Explain to participants the following ideas, which are relevant when working to assess children in relation to a court case.

Confidentiality

Start by explaining to the child that you need to know about their wishes and feelings so you can make safe plans for them. Tell the child what you are going to tell the grown-ups or court.

You can say something like:

I cannot keep secrets about you not being safe or about you being hurt. If I feel that you are not safe or you have been hurt, then it is my job to keep you safe by telling the court (judge) (explain what a judge is).

A helpful story here is one that we will look at in Session 2, *The river of happy and sad and lonely feelings*; another is the *Seed story*. These stories explain why the court might be involved in the child's situation.

Using time well

Say to participants that, when ascertaining a child's wishes and feelings in relation to court work, we often have limited time, so using various assessment techniques (which will be described in Session 2) can help you obtain information quickly.

One way to introduce a technique is to suggest to the child that they play one of their games followed by one of yours. End with one of *their* games.

For children under the age of eight, use puppets or a toy telephone and talk through it, or use a favourite attachment toy. At this point demonstrate this to participants using something like a puppet, teddy bear or tortoise:

- 'Can you tell Teddy why you were sad?', or
- Talk to Teddy yourself saying, 'Teddy, Sean seems sad. Do you think he could tell *you* how he is feeling?'
- Take your eye contact away from the child so they can tell Teddy something without inhibition.

  Forms of questioning:

- "What" and "How" questions are most useful.
- "Why" is a less useful question, since the child is unlikely to know the answer!
- "Where" could cause the child to feel pressure if they think you are trying to prise information from them.

  Stress that in social work we have to be *very* careful not to lead the child via questions or games. Remember with children always to use open-ended questions, i.e. not ones that lead to a "yes" or "no" answer. You should also avoid directing them to answer in a particular way.

Listening empathetically

Explain that empathetic listening in this context is rather like being a sports commentator "noticing" or "tracking" what is happening. This means not judging but simply taking note of what the child is doing and saying about what is happening. They will tell you or show you their meaning if they can.

The aim here is simply to find themes and patterns from what we hear, not to impose our values or judgements on them.

For example, as the child plays with the toys, comment on what's happening, "notice" and say, for instance:

- 'The red car is following the green car.'
- 'Oh! The car crashed,' heightening your tone as you say this.
- The child might say 'The man's dead,' and you might respond: 'Poor man,' lowering your tone softly.
- Repeat what you heard the child say and then ask, 'What happened next?'; the child will often elaborate.
- Then say, 'Wow, what a story!' In this way you are not leading but the child feels heard.

Prompting expansion

Explain that you can invite a child to expand on a point by using enquiry, such as:

- I am wondering if you would like to choose...?' or 'I am wondering if you feel he's lost or...'

If a child is playing with dolls or animals you could say:

- Can you show and tell me how the story went?'

Then, if they are stuck, say:

- What happened next?'

If the story then stops, say:

- Wow, what a story! Thank you for sharing that with me.'

Reflecting feelings

Explain that you can do this by, for example, saying:

- 'Ouch, ouch!' if Teddy gets hurt
- 'You did enjoy that!' upping your tone of voice, 'How did you feel?'
- 'It sounds as if you're finding this really painful,' offering a cuddly toy to hug.

When noticing a child's play, interject to show sincere interest by using phrases such as:

- 'Really?'
- 'I see!'
- 'That's interesting.'
- 'That's fun.'
- 'Oh, how sad.'
- 'Would you like to tell me about it?'
- 'Can you tell me what else happened?'
- 'Seems you had some mixed feelings about that...'
- 'I was wondering how...'
- 'Was anyone else around when that happened?' Or 'Was there anyone there to keep you safe?'
- 'I can see you want me to know how hard you are trying,' or 'You are working really hard to fix that'. When they have fixed whatever it is, say 'You must feel very proud' and smile at them.

17   **EXERCISE: LISTENING THROUGH PLAY**

SAND TRAY WORK

The aim of this particular exercise is to teach participants how to use a third object such as a toy or button to describe their family in the sand tray as if they were using a standard eco-map. If you need to describe what an eco-map is, use Handout 1.3 to describe one. You should also give out Handout 1.8 on listening skills at this point.

Explain that, although eco-maps on paper serve a useful function, they just generate a cognitive response. By using a sand tray (as described earlier) to make an eco-map you will reach the emotional memory of the child much more quickly and you will therefore be able to discover what the child really feels about the members of their family.

Say that you will now ask participants to experience what it is like to use a sand tray as a form of eco-map.

- Give each person a paper plate with a little sand on it. (This is a substitute for a real sand tray.)
- Tell participants they will need to select some of the toys they have brought in order to describe their birth family or to illustrate a family day out. The aim is for them to do this as a child would see the situation – using sand will help them do this.
- Explain that this exercise demonstrates how objects or toys give us privacy and take some of the pain out of the telling of something difficult. For example:
  - Mum could be represented by a toy cooker because she was always cooking, or as a mother animal.
  - Dad could be an "armchair" because he read the paper all the time, or a lion because he seemed to be in charge.
  - Aunt could be a "wall" made in sand because she doesn't speak to anyone.
- Explain that in feedback you won't be asking what was discussed, but only how well the technique worked.
- Ask participants to get into pairs and work together on this, with each participant spending 10 minutes using the listening skills described previously. For example, say that the listener should start by saying:

'Only share what you feel comfortable sharing' and then

'Can you make me a picture in the sand?' or

'Can you make me a picture of a family day out?'

'Tell and show me your story.'

Remind participants that the listener should remember to be a "feelings commentator" (like a sports commentator). Listeners should not judge. They are only there to take note of what the child says about what is happening. They will tell you or show you if they can. We are only looking for themes and patterns in what we hear, not imposing our values or judgements.

When the time is up, get the group back together to feed back and discuss.

Ask participants the following:

- Did you feel that you had told the listener more about yourself than you expected?

- Did you remember to put yourself into the sand tray?
- Did you notice whether your perception of characters in your family was different from what it is now? (Vera Fahlberg (1994) points out that our perception of the world changes at the ages of 3, 5, 7, 11 and 14 years, and so on.)
- What did you think the sand was for?

Explain that sensory stimulation on the fingertips (via the sand) evokes early sensory and visual memories. A child can also use it to bury people they miss, don't like or are frightened of.

Say that, if when using this technique a child describes being left or hurt, you can ask a child if there was anyone there to help.

If your course participants are parents and carers who will be using this technique, explain that they can ask questions if they are just playing with the child. However, if they are using this technique in a "special playtime" (as in filial play), they should remain non-directive and just note what is happening.

Explain to participants that in Session 2 we will be doing a follow-on game to this one.

10 minutes   **18   CLOSING THE SESSION**

If you have time, ask whether one of the participants would like to read an extract from pp. 66–70 in *The Little Prince* by Antoine De Saint-Exupéry, which is about taming and making relationships. Explain that using stories is a very good way to sum up the main theme of a day or a play session with a child without directly going over the lesson again.

Suggest to participants that, in order to consolidate today's learning, they should read the summary on p. 22 in Chapter 2: *Attachment* in the *Handbook*.

Tell participants that in Session 2 we will be looking at children's grief, managing difficult feelings and making a good assessment.

SESSION 2
Managing difficult feelings and making good assessments

OVERVIEW

	Section	Timing
1	Welcome	**10 minutes**
2	Exercise: *Driving game*	**20 minutes**
3	Goals for Session 2	**5 minutes**
4	Presentation: *Looking at grief* Exercise: *How to help a child become emotionally unstuck*	**75 minutes**
5	Break	**15 minutes**
6	Presentation: *Helping children to manage strong feelings* Exercise: *Anger and its meaning*	**30 minutes**
7	Presentation: *Looking at angry behaviour in children* Exercise: *Practical techniques for handling anger*	**55 minutes**
8	Lunch	**1 hour**
9	Introducing a framework for working with vulnerable children	**10 minutes**
10	Exercise: *Jacob's case study*	**30 minutes**
11	Basic assessment questions	**20 minutes**
12	Break	**15 minutes**
13	Practical session on using assessment techniques	**45 minutes**
14	Exercises: *Assessing parenting styles and identifying children's attachment figures*	**15 minutes**
15	Summarising assessments in reports	**10 minutes**
16	Closing the session	**5 minutes**

Note: If you are running this course only for people intending to adopt (i.e. rather than for social workers and foster carers as well), you may feel that the material covered after lunch is not particularly relevant for your participants. If this is the case, then at this point in Session 2 you should start using material from Session 3, taking more time over some of the exercises or adding more from the *Techniques CD*. (Having said this, in my experience I have found that whatever group I have been teaching has usually found at least some of the material provided after lunch in Session 2 useful.)

PREPARATION

In preparation for delivering and adding to the presentations below, read Chapters 2–9 in the *Handbook* and familiarise yourself with the techniques in the corresponding chapters on the *Techniques CD*.

PARTICULAR RESOURCES NEEDED FOR THIS SESSION

- An animal glove puppet
- Sample copies of various books recommended during the day – in particular, *Muddles, Puddles and Sunshine*, published by Winston's Wish (and available from Winston's Wish) and *Managing Difficult Behaviour* (Pallett *et al*, 2006)
- A balloon and biro for each participant
- The *Bears* cards (available from BAAF)
- The Barnardo's *All about me* game – this is very expensive but worth mentioning because of its excellence as an assessment tool
- Jacob's case study – only one copy for yourself
- A range of equipment, such as slimes, oozes, balls or beanbags, modelling clay, tiddlywinks, fingerpaints, etc, for trying out techniques for managing anger. See the *Techniques CD* under *Play equipment and materials.*

HANDOUTS

- 2.1 Session 2: overview
- 2.2 *Grief curve and instruction*
- 2.3 *Jacob's case study*
- 2.4 *Quick reference assessment questions*
- 2.5 *Demonstration flowchart*
- 2.6 *The river of happy and sad and lonely feelings*
- 2.7 *The seed story*
- 2.8 *Cartoon pictures with instruction sheet*
- 2.9 *Feelings faces*
- 2.10 *Sand tray stories*
- 2.11 *The window exercise*
- 2.12 *Parent message cards and instructions*
- Copies for each participant of Session 2's PowerPoint presentation slides

10 minutes

1 WELCOME

- Welcome participants and explain that during the morning of this second session you will be looking at the subjects of handling grief and managing strong feelings and that this afternoon they will have the opportunity to practise more assessment techniques and ideas.
- Remind participants of the house rules concerning confidentiality.
- Give a quick summary of what the group learnt in Session 1, i.e. the interface between attachment, trauma and loss in the context of normal child development, as well as how to make a start on working with children, how to engage children and young people, setting up a session, and use of a third object.
- Ask if anyone had any thoughts, as a result of Session 1, that they want to share, and allow five minutes for them to do this.
- Show Slide 1.

20 minutes **2** **EXERCISE: DRIVING GAME**

The aim of this exercise is to get participants working as a group together in order to demonstrate how hard it can be for a child and parent/carer to trust and understand each other.

SLIDE 1
Managing difficult feelings and making good assessments

Explain Game No. 2, the driving game, using the instructions on the *Techniques CD.*

● Ask participants to stand up and choose a partner.
● Choose someone you can demonstrate the following on.
  – Ask him or her to stand in front of you, saying: 'You are going to be a car and I am going to be the driver.'
  – Ask the person to close their eyes as you explain the rules. Say, 'When I put my hand between your shoulder blades you walk forward. If I want you to stop, I will press firmly with my fingertips. To turn right, I will tap on your right shoulder and to turn left, I will tap on your left shoulder.'
  – Move them around the room for about two minutes doing this.
● Then ask the group in their partners to choose who is going to be the driver first. Remind those who are the cars to close their eyes. Tell drivers to then navigate the car round the room without giving any instructions while trying not to bump into each other. Stop them all after two minutes.

Ask participants how it felt to be the cars. Then ask the drivers what their experiences were.

The answers given are likely to include: being nervous or not understanding the rules (especially if you are finding it takes time to get the hang of them); feeling frightened of crashing; being unsure as to whether one could trust the driver; feeling tempted to cheat and take control; not really understanding how to execute the rules; feeling confidence in the driver.

Then ask the partners to swap roles, and spend a further two minutes playing the game.

Then ask for feedback as before.

Finally, end the exercise by explaining that the point of it was to learn:

● how it feels for children and their carers getting to know each other when coming into care or going to permanent families;
● how hard it is for children to understand the new rules they experience in a different setting;
● how hard it is for carers to help children to feel comfortable in a new setting and to understand the child's reactions to the rules, especially when the child is going through a grieving process;
● how frustrating it feels for carers when one cannot get the child to understand their family's rules, expectations and culture. It's all about trust and how hard it can be to do this for both parties.

Then ask the whole group to take their seats again.

5 minutes   **3   GOALS FOR SESSION 2**

Go through the points on Slide 2, explaining what the goals of the session will be, referring to the Notes.

SLIDE 2
Goals for Session 2

- Helping children express and process grief
- Assessment of wishes and feelings
- Managing strong emotions and behaviours

75 minutes   **4   PRESENTATION: LOOKING AT GRIEF**

Explain to participants that the techniques looked at in this part of the course are very powerful and that the material will stir up feelings of loss in us all. This might make them feel that they want to talk about their feelings, but they should only share what they will later feel comfortable with having shared. If at any point such feelings become overwhelming, invite participants to talk to you, as trainer, and/or sit out of any exercises they feel unable to participate in.

Explain that loss and trauma underpin most of the experiences of children in the care system, and that they are thus usually processing loss at some level. The different behaviours they show are often a manifestation of their particular experience of grief or trauma, or their attachment style.

During any assessment of a child's behaviour we also need to consider his or her temperament and talents, and the individual developmental milestones they have reached. To do this you will need to think about and observe the child's behaviour, as well as taking note of what the family or carer says about that child's temperament.

The six stages of loss, and the effects of secondary trauma

Before showing Slide 3, explain that Elisabeth Kübler-Ross was a doctor who cared for the dying and who produced the findings of her research on death and dying in a social science paper in 1969, which later developed into a very famous book on the subject.

Kübler-Ross identified the stages people go through in coming to terms with and processing grief as being:

- Denial
- Isolation
- Anger
- Bargaining
- Depression
- Acceptance

Claudia Jewett, in her book *Separation and Loss* (1984), also outlines these stages in similar terms.

Show Slide 3.

SLIDE 3
Loss and separation

Stage 1: Immobility, shock and numbing
Stage 2: Depression, denial and disbelief
Stage 3: Underestimation, yearning and pining: Anger, shame and guilt
Stage 4: Despair: "The pits"
Stage 5: Discovery, recognition
Stage 6: Revitalisation

(Adapted from Kubler-Ross (1969)/Jewett (1984))

As participants look at Slide 3, distribute Handout 2.2 which shows the grief curve. Explain that the stages shown on Slide 3 are a useful tool that participants can photocopy and use with their clients to help them understand where they or their child is at present on the grief curve. (As mentioned in Session 1, sometimes children can get emotionally "stuck" between Stages 3 and 4, but they can recover if helped to become "unstuck".)

Then explain that Slide 4 shows the same diagram as one they saw in the previous session. This shows the grief process as being divided into negative and positive stages, with the carer/parents holding the secondary trauma and experiencing the pain of the child – which can become overwhelming if this pain is similar to the carer/parent's own childhood experience which they have not yet resolved.

Briefly remind participants of the explanation of the six-stage model given in Session 1 and refer to the Notes to amplify this.

SLIDE 4
The six-stage model of bereavement and the effects of secondary trauma

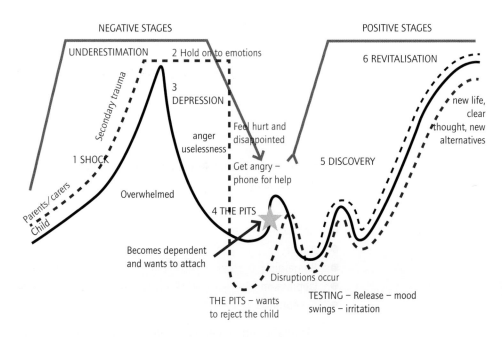

EXERCISE: HOW TO HELP A CHILD BECOME EMOTIONALLY UNSTUCK

Display Slide 3 again and say that you will now be doing an exercise designed to explore how to help a child become emotionally unstuck – if this has happened to them – for example, during Stages 3 and 4.

Divide the group into smaller groups of equal numbers, in which participants can start thinking about how to help children through grief and to come up with their own ideas.

- Draw attention to the six stages of grief on Slide 3 and then write the following questions on the flipchart:
  1. How do children show grief at each stage of the grieving process?
  2. What could we, or carers, do in our practice to help the child at each stage?

- Ask each group to write down the headings and make a list under each of the stages for Question 1.
- Say that they should then discuss and write down their suggestions to Question 2.
- Tell participants that they will have 30 minutes in which to do the exercise.

Feedback

Ask the groups to give their feedback to the larger group in turn, a stage at a time. As they go through their feedback, add anything you think they may have left out, referring to the notes in the *Handbook* in Chapter 4: *Grief and Loss* under the 'How can we help?' headings for each stage (or on the *Techniques CD*).

When you are taking feedback on Stage 3 of the grieving process (anger, shame and guilt), tell participants that you will shortly be looking at this in more detail after the feedback on this exercise has been completed.

Carry on taking feedback on this exercise and, when you have finished, talk through Stage 3 of the grieving process, using Slide 5.

Exploring Stage 3 of the grieving process: Anger, shame and guilt

Now show Slide 5.

SLIDE 5
Anger, shame and guilt

- Children who are traumatised can become very angry, hurt and confused: they try to protect themselves against the huge world.
- They feel powerless: they try to be powerful and to draw attention to their powerlessness by angry, aggressive behaviour.
- As a result they have powerful feelings of shame and guilt.
- In extreme cases, these feelings get turned inwards and the child becomes self-harming.

To explain the differences between guilt and shame, refer to the Notes accompanying the slide.

Explain that, in order to help children deal with these strong feelings, the adult has to allow and encourage the child to accept these feelings – and in order to accept one's feelings, one needs to be helped to recognise them via their senses and to feel them in the first place.

You can demonstrate how this can be done either by using a puppet (that you brought with you) while telling the following case study, or, if you prefer, using a case study from your own experience.

CASE STUDY

Jan, a foster carer, is sitting next to George, who is aged six. He has been miserable all day and cannot speak. She picks up her special listening dog puppet that sits on the sofa and starts to talk to it. She addresses the dog: 'Listening dog,' she says, 'George is very sad today but he can't tell me how he's feeling. Do you think he would be able to talk to you about what's worrying him?' She then puts the puppet in front of George and says in the voice of the puppet, 'Do you want to tell me what's up?'

Young children will often suspend their disbelief and chat away on a toy phone or to a bear or puppet as long as they don't have to have eye contact with the adult involved. The same is true of young people. They will often use a favourite bear or chat from the back of the car, as long as they don't feel they are being questioned.

Children's grief is like "muddles, puddles and sunshine", a phrase used as the title of a book published by the charity Winston's Wish. This is an excellent book on helping children when they have lost a parent to death, but is also helpful for children in care. (The title describes how children's experience of loss is like jumping into puddles: one minute they feel really sad, the next they feel OK and can play.) At this point you should draw participants' attention to the book list at the back of the *Handbook*.

Explain that later this morning, after the break, participants will be able to practise more techniques to help manage difficult feelings. The listening techniques taught in Session 1 are also helpful in these situations. Remind participants that this means doing things like the following when assessing a child:

● Notice what the child is doing and comment on it like a "sports commentator", saying things like:
  – 'The doll is tucked up in bed so cosily.'
● Then reflect the feelings. If, for example, the child pretends to cry for the doll, the listener says, 'Oh, the baby is sad or maybe hungry.'

Other factors affecting how a child copes with grief

Mention that other factors will affect how a child copes with the various stages of the grieving process, including the following.

● The child's experience of attachment and other relationships: An anxious child who is not sure if their birth parent really cared for them will blame themselves for the loss of their parent, saying things like, 'I can't have been good enough'. An avoidant child will say, 'I don't care anyway, he was nasty'.
● The age, sex, temperament, intellectual stage of the child and their social circumstances before and after separation will affect the child's manifestation of loss. Cultural expectations (for example, the way in which a funeral was conducted) can vary widely as each of the world religions has different customs and traditions about saying goodbye to their next of

kin, as well as about the funeral and the length of time the family is expected to mourn. For instance, in most of the main religions there is the belief that when a person dies a part of them (referred to as the soul) lives in another place. Hindus, Sikhs and Buddhists believe that people are reincarnated, i.e. their souls may return many times as a new person before going to heaven. However, Jews, Christians and Muslims believe you can only live on earth once and God decides what happens to you. Advise participants to seek out children's library books to help them better understand the traditions of various different faiths.

- The child's "cognitive appraisal" of the loss, i.e. their perception of the event, such as it meaning that they have to go to a new school, or their understanding of how the parent was lost. Cognitive appraisal means the child's internal voice explaining what has happened to them (which may be a fantasy rather than reality).
- The child's "cognitive set": this refers to their sense of self-esteem and their ability to think for themselves.
- A child's previous experience of losses that occurred before the present loss could also affect their reaction, i.e. if earlier losses weren't dealt with thoroughly on previous occasions then hopelessness and helplessness can become the predominant feature in subsequent losses.
- The reason for the separation: what the home environment was like before they came in to care, i.e. if the child had been neglected, they won't have an expectation of care or nurture.
- Unresolved earlier grief: the present separation may trigger grief from a previous, more important loss that has never been resolved (like the loss of a grandparent).
- The carer's own unresolved grief: sometimes when a child is placed with new parents who have experienced their own major loss or trauma, those new parents may not yet have dealt with their own grief. The adult's own grief curve (secondary trauma) (as shown on Slide 4) then runs just behind the child's, often causing the adult to panic and become paralysed in their effort to rescue, heal or comfort. This then keeps the child in an emotionally stuck state.

Suggest to participants that certain books can offer practical help when working with children who have experienced loss and are grieving. As before, point out the following books in the book list at the end of the *Handbook.*

- *Managing Difficult Behaviour: Tips and techniques*
- *Muddles, Puddles and Sunshine*
- *Helping Children with Loss: A guide book*
- *Helping Children with Separation and Loss*

End this presentation by covering any of the material given below in the "Final points" section that you have not yet covered. These are all important things to remember when dealing with loss and separation. You can also ask for any further points from participants' own lists written on the flipchart during the earlier exercise.

Final points

- It is important to help children listen to their feelings without judging them as good and bad – it is OK to feel as we feel. When talking to a child dealing with loss, try to say things like 'How sad' or 'It's so hard when you miss people', and raise the emotional tone of your voice. We cannot make a child feel better instantly or rescue them from their sadness, but we can allow them to feel this sadness by staying with them in their pain and responding empathetically. We can then eventually reflect back what they have said or ask them if they can think of a different ending to their story, which can then help them to see hope. A child may at first repeat the same story about a loss over and over again in story form, i.e. they always die or never win.

Using the same metaphor, the worker can "wonder" if there might be a different ending, thus helping the child explore the possibility of resolution or recovery from loss.

- Losing someone or something is very painful and a big shock. Children can often feel it's their fault that they have lost their mum or dad. Try to let the child know that they shouldn't tell themselves off because it's *not* their fault. Listen to what the child has said and reflect back the overall feeling when they appear to have finished sharing. Then give them something to do that affirms them in one of their competencies (for example, drawing or later on swimming or riding a bike).

- Children need to know that it's OK to cry – in fact, that it's normal and very brave to cry. Children or young people can often tell who's good at listening, and whom they feel safe to be with when they are sad or want to cry. Suggest the child looks for comfort from someone whom they can feel safe with and who is kind and gentle: mummy or grandparents, foster mum, teddy, etc.

- Children can be helped to see that loss is like jumping into puddles: one minute they feel really sad, the next they feel OK and can play. Children can be reassured that it's perfectly OK to feel this way. When you lose someone you love, the world can become cold and grey. If you can tell someone you trust how you feel and get them to listen, they will comfort you and understand how strong your feelings are.

- It's important to allow a grieving child to let out their anger because deeper sorrow is often hidden below this fury. This can be done through using "angry box techniques". This involves using the senses to recover feelings and to re-nurture the body – for example, cooking, playing with warm water or warm play dough, or stroking a pet or furry toy. Such sensory material will open up the emotional and sensory memory and help the child feel again after a traumatic event or loss. In this way they can become emotionally unstuck, begin to heal, and find the words for their feelings so that they can get their needs met and communicate successfully with adults. Smelling clothes that belong to the lost person and looking at photos will all help a child in this stage of grief to let go slowly. As the child experiences feelings again, they may show agitation or anger. As we have discussed, dealing with these feeling as the child expresses them allows the child to progress to the positive stages of grief. Once you've done this in a session with a child, it's helpful to encourage a simple and normal activity that reminds the child of their competence, thus giving scaffolding on which to build and encouraging hope that the world is still there for them to explore – only this time it's with a *new* secure base, their new carer.

- Explain that there are positive points that can be made to children about the grieving process:
  - Recovering from loss takes a long time. Hurting, or accepting it has happened, is all part of the cure and these are therefore helpful experiences.
  - When we lose loved people we have memories in us about them. Eventually these memories about loved, lost people will warm and comfort us when we think of them. These memories are what make us into the people we are and make us feel strong and able to tackle adversity when we feel down. This is called "resilience" (see Chapter 4 in the *Handbook* for more on this important subject).
  - We can become the "hero of our own story". As the child plays out stories about heroes and heroines who rescue or kill the dragon, etc., in their own play, they too are recovering from loss or trauma and this is a useful way to boost their self-esteem. You can say, 'You know you are the hero of your own life story, and have survived.'
  - If you have loved someone deeply, it will hurt more when you lose them, so if it's really painful now, it means you had the courage to love someone really well and that they will have felt loved, which is the greatest gift you can give someone.

– As a child recovers from loss, this shows that over time they have benefited from the warmth of the people and good things on the planet around them. The carer needs to notice that they have become curious once again and want to learn new things, and that this shows they are recovering. Try to celebrate their recovery with them and review the past, emphasising their achievements.

After going through these points, tell participants that after the break you will be trying out new ideas about how to help with a child's strong feelings if they come up in an interview or just at home when children are stressed.

15 minutes	**5**	**BREAK**

30 minutes   **6**   **PRESENTATION: HELPING CHILDREN TO MANAGE STRONG FEELINGS**

Show Slide 6 and explain the parent/carer intervention cycle in it, using the Notes.

In all relationships between parents and children, parents soothe and regulate a child through the use of nurture and healthy socialisation (for example, hugs and clear, non-harsh boundaries). Parents and carers can help in grief by being alongside the child. They have to remain a secure base and at the same time realise that they can't hurry grief: each child needs to go at their own pace. However, this does not mean they should let all boundaries go or stop nurturing the child, even when they are challenging or distressed.

SLIDE 6
Parent/ carer intervention cycle

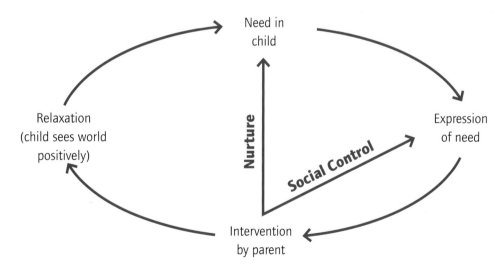

Helps child to regulate feelings

(Based on the arousal-relaxation cycle by Fahlberg, 1994)

Now go on to show participants Slide 7, which outlines the process of a child getting in touch with their feelings, a process necessary when doing direct work with a child.

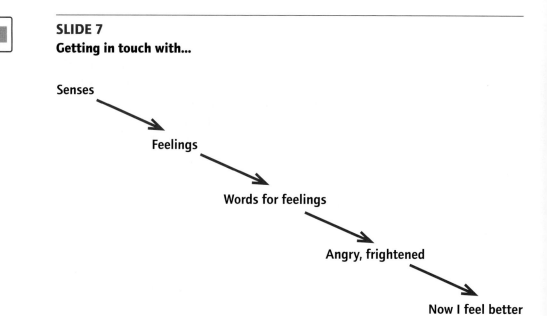

SLIDE 7
Getting in touch with...

Senses

Feelings

Words for feelings

Angry, frightened

Now I feel better

Then introduce Slide 8, which looks at how to prepare a play session with a child during which you may have to manage difficult feelings.

SLIDE 8
The session

● Go at the pace of the child
● Allow the child time to examine and explore
● Use a third object to open communication

Explain that, before starting work on grief, it is important to remind oneself about listening skills, confidentiality and boundaries.

Say that, when you are going through a session with a child, you will probably want to record what happens. You can tell the child that you will write their story down in this little book and that they can write in it too if they would like to. Often a child likes to actually draw things on your notes and this can help further our understanding of their wishes and feelings.

Explain that many people find it hard to manage strong feelings in any kind of situation, whether in the family or in an interview. For this reason, before looking at assessment in detail, we will consider the subject of dealing with anger, since this is often the reason why clients challenge us, or that a child's behaviour is regarded as being poor. A painful situation can often act as a trigger to an outburst of anger or can open up a difficult situation. The next exercise looks at this.

EXERCISE: ANGER AND ITS MEANING

Write the following questions on the flipchart.

● What indications are there in terms of behaviour when someone is angry?
● What are the functions of anger, i.e. what might it be trying to communicate?

- What might its appearance signify in terms of what a child is feeling?

Ask participants to get into small groups to discuss these questions. Tell them that they have 15 minutes in which to do this.

After 15 minutes, ask for feedback of their ideas and write these down on the flipchart.

Then show them Slide 9, which offers some ideas they may not have come up with.

SLIDE 9
What is anger?

- An inability to tolerate discomfort and a consequent tension release
- A mask for other emotions, i.e. fear, jealousy, sadness, loneliness, helplessness
- A stage in grief processing
- A difficult emotion that gets turned inwards and becomes depression
- A separation technique used when one is feeling too dependent
- An attempt to make physical contact with a person
- A reaction to feeling unheard or misunderstood
- A learned response, e.g. fighting has become the learned pattern of behaviour in reaction to certain situations
- A projection or reflection, for example, 'I feel bad: it's you that's making me feel bad and therefore I am angry with you' (projection)
- Reflection: copying the behaviour of parents

---

55 minutes

7   PRESENTATION: LOOKING AT ANGRY BEHAVIOUR IN CHILDREN

Explain to participants that all those working with children facing loss and trauma have to know how to manage powerful feelings so that the child feels safe to express them.

The following points may or may not have come up when doing the earlier exercise on anger, but if any of them haven't been covered, then you should use them as an introduction to the work on practical techniques that comes next.

Explain to participants that:

- Children have trouble in expressing anger but it is important to get them to do so because under a layer of angry feelings are hurt feelings that also need to be accessed. Also, when anger is suppressed it is often then displaced, i.e. expressed in other ways. It is therefore very helpful to give children opportunities to express anger safely.
- Angry children are not popular with adults because their behaviour disrupts the social situation in which most people feel comfortable. There is therefore a real danger of adults starting to identify children with their angry behaviour and then rejecting them totally, so that angry children then feel unloved in themselves. Many children come into care because of this type of rejection. Unfortunately, usually the same pattern is reinforced while they are in care.
- Angry behaviour in children also occurs within a system that has double standards for adults and children. For instance, an adult may interrupt a child, but a child may not interrupt an adult.
- Children feel that adulthood is a long way off, and this may make them want to rush ahead of the appropriate stages of their development. This means they try to do adult things before they are emotionally ready to do them and then, because they can't actually do whatever it

is, they become angry, frustrated and defiant. They are trying to mirror adults' behaviour but emotionally can't cope with doing so. This is often an inappropriate attempt beyond their years to control adults.

- Children behaving aggressively or destructively are often insecure, anxious, hurt and suffering from a diffused sense of self, often because of poor attachment experience. Their low opinion of themselves makes them fearful of expressing their real feelings and so they resort to anger. In some family situations they may have to repress their anger, which then can lead to sadness, apathy and depression or controlling behaviours.

Dealing with strong feelings

- The first step is for the worker to show respect for the child by listening reflectively. Then he or she must try to reach the deeper feelings hidden by the anger, such as abandonment or loss.
- Offer an activity to express anger like "scribble drawing" or to help release the sadness. Or, as discussed in Session 1, listen reflectively by tracking what the child is doing (e.g. when working with a sand tray) while they do it.
- Give children practical means whereby they can express their anger, i.e. by using techniques such as the following, which participants will be introduced to in the next exercise.
  - helping them to recognise the actual feeling of anger that they are experiencing – naming it;
  - showing them how to express their angry feelings verbally and directly to the person they need to express them to when it's safe to do so;
  - rehearsing this through the use of story and play.
- Talk with children about anger – what it is, what makes them angry, how they can show it, what they can do when they feel it. This is particularly effectively done when the child is NOT angry. This can also be done by using metaphor via a fairy story (such as the one mentioned in the *Handbook,* Chapter 9: *Therapeutic stories*).
- Help children to see that *everyone* feels angry sometimes, and that anger can be healthy, e.g. there can be righteous anger about an injustice.

EXERCISE: PRACTICAL TECHNIQUES FOR HANDLING ANGER

From the 'Games and techniques for helping children express anger' given below (which is taken from the *Techniques CD*), choose four or five ideas to demonstrate how children can be helped to express anger. Then get participants to try them out. Explain to participants that all of these techniques can also be really helpful for parents to use.

For example:

- You could start this exercise by showing participants how to do "scribble drawings", then demonstrate one or two, and end with everyone doing the balloon fights. You should give participants coloured pens and paper with which to do these drawings and then use the instructions to be found on the *Techniques CD*, in Chapter 6: *Assessment.*
- Once participants have made a scribble drawing, show them how to use slime and ooze. Having shown the case study under scribble drawings, demonstrate how slime and ooze can be dropped over a scribble drawing. Say that a child can be invited to throw slime, etc., over a picture they have drawn. This can be a really useful way for a child to let go in a manageable, sensory and fun way, and their desire to do this will demonstrate how much they need to let go at that point.

Whichever techniques you choose to demonstrate to participants, allow 30 minutes to give you time to demonstrate them first and then for participants to try them.

Explain to participants that all the techniques can be found on the *Techniques CD*.

Games and techniques for helping children express anger

Now demonstrate or explain to participants the games from the following list that you have decided to show them within the time you have left.

- Calming visualisation for parents: This is an exercise to calm the self, and which enables one to calm a client. Demonstrate this using the technique described in No. 27 on the *Techniques CD*, in *Grief and loss*.
- Bells/drums/foot stamping/angry-sounding music: You could work with a child by getting them to, for example, bang a drum, and then you can mirror their emotions demonstrated on the drum by doing the same yourself on another instrument.
- Using puppets: These can be useful for expressing powerful feelings. For example, you can use a dragon puppet to show how one can turn their fire on or off, which is a good metaphor for showing that one can control one's own strong feelings. Remember that if you use animal puppets such as dragons, lizards or crocodiles you shouldn't assume that these are scary or bad in the children's minds. Make sure you ask the child what type of character *they* think the animal has and how the character feels – it could be an angry lion or a friendly lion like Simba in *The Lion King*. The child needs to tell you: you cannot presume the nature of the animal's character.
- Beanbag, punch bag or trampoline for the child: Use these when exercise is needed to dispel both frustration and cortisol (which, if allowed to build up, will result in angry outbursts that the child can't control and will be frightened of, as well as making those around him frightened).
- Calm sitting/with music: See "warning cards" for children who don't respond to reward systems. This is explained on the *Techniques CD*, No. 19, in *Neglect and trauma*.
- Breathing out the anger: This is done by counting from 0 to 5 and inhaling slowly before repeating.
- Scribble drawing (Game No. 30)/empowerment games: These are explained on the *Techniques CD* in *Neglect and trauma*, *Grief and loss* and *Assessment*.
- Use of slime and ooze: see earlier.
- Clay modelling/papier mâché: These can be used to make volcanoes with "feeling rocks" that the child can destroy: see the instructions on the *Techniques CD*, Game No. 38, in *Assessing needs, wishes and feelings*.
- Painting feelings of rage: It can be useful to do this using finger paints as this will stimulate the child's senses, thus helping them to get in touch with their feelings.
- Water game (Game No. 81): You should demonstrate this one fully later in today's session. For instructions see the *Techniques CD*.
- Sand tray work: As described in Session 1 and in Game No. 41 on the *Techniques CD*.
- Frustration box: This is helpful when used with special "time out space" – see Game No. 28 on the *Techniques CD*.
- Counters game: See Game No. 23 on the *Techniques CD*.

- Monster games (Game No. 25): See the book, *If I Turned Into a Monster*, in the book list on the *Techniques CD*.
- Domino game: see Game No. 24 on the *Techniques CD*.

The balloon fight game

End this exercise by getting participants to do the following (although before you start, find out if any participants dislike balloons – in which case, suggest they sit out). See Game No. 20 on the *Techniques CD*.

- Give each person a balloon.
- Ask them to blow up the balloon.
- Then ask them to draw an angry face on the balloon.
- Tell them to have a balloon fight with a neighbour.
- Get them all to pop the balloons at the same time using a biro. As the balloon shrivels up, say 'Notice how small your angry face has got as the balloon shrivels up'. Playing or talking about strong feelings makes these feelings smaller, like the balloon face.

Explain that you should do this about three times with children so the child begins to lets go of all their stored cortisol and it disperses, ending with them making happy face balloons that they *don't* pop and then with them choosing an activity they like doing.

Summary of work on anger

Explain that, by using techniques such as those just described, as well as reflective listening, we can enable children to feel free enough, yet sufficiently contained, to safely express their strong feelings. In this way they can grieve for lost nurturing, and adjust and get perspective on the loss or trauma that they may have endured.

However, if we repress these feelings and *stop* children feeling, they cannot learn to manage their own behaviour and will have poor maturation of the social emotions, i.e. empathy, pride, guilt, shame and embarrassment. If children don't develop an ability to regulate their own emotions, they cannot form a conscience and show other people that they care and would like to be friends with them. If a child is not able to express or feel these emotions, he or she can become depressed, have violent outbursts and ultimately develop mental health issues.

Suggest that participants might like to do some further reading using the list of children's story books that appears at the end of the *Techniques CD*.

In addition, here are some useful titles, full details of which can be found in the book list in the *Handbook*:

- *Managing Difficult Behaviour*
- *Beyond Consequences and Control*
- Various books by Caroline Archer mentioned on the *Techniques CD*

1 hour   **8   LUNCH**

10 minutes   **9   INTRODUCING A FRAMEWORK FOR WORKING WITH VULNERABLE CHILDREN**

Before presenting this section you will need to have read and be familiar with Chapter 6: *Assessing children's needs, wishes and feelings* in the *Handbook.*

Explain that this afternoon you will be going on to look at "direct work" assessment techniques. (This is because this course is teaching the use of direct work as a means of ascertaining the wishes and feelings of a child facing a change.)

At this point, show Slide 10 and once it has been read, say that you will return to this at the end of the afternoon. Displaying the slide now briefly shows participants the purpose of direct work assessment.

SLIDE 10
Direct work assessment

- Look for themes and patterns of how the child sees their world, and how they express their wishes and feelings.
- Notice how they make relationships and the nature of these.
- Are there any developmental delays?
- What is their experience of trauma and loss?

For each of the above, you need three pieces of evidence from your direct work.

Say that, before doing this, you will show a framework that has been created to guide the worker in deciding when it would be helpful to do particular aspects of their direct work with children facing change.

Introduce Slide 11 at this point and talk through the notes accompanying the slide.

SLIDE 11
A framework for direct work with children

- Assessment
- Transitional support: grief, identity, self-esteem
- Repair: life history
- Moving without trauma: repair
- Repair: re-attachment

30 minutes   **10   EXERCISE: JACOB'S CASE STUDY**

For this exercise you will need Handout 2.3, *Jacob's case study.*

- Ask participants to look at Handout 2.3, *Jacob's case study.*
- Then play the game.
- Then ask for feedback of any feelings this aroused in the group.
- Then put up Slide 12 and get participants to answers these questions in groups.

SLIDE 12
Jacob's case study

What practice issues did this game highlight?

What, in your one-to-one assessment of him, do you think Jacob needs to know?

Share ideas about how you might find out what you need to know in play or chat with him.

What information do you need to find out about him to complete an assessment? Make a list.

Feedback on exercise

Once you have the feedback from participants, record it on the flipchart. Then explain that you will now be looking through a series of slides covering basic assessment questions.

20 minutes   **11   BASIC ASSESSMENT QUESTIONS**

Before presenting the next few slides, use extra material in the *Handbook* in Chapter 6: *Assessing children's needs, wishes and feelings*, p. 66, to expand on the presentation (summarised below).

- What we are looking for?
- Attachment – recognising signals
- Developmental delay and specific difficulties
- Loss and trauma
- Identity, ethnicity, religion and culture
- Disability, physical, mental and emotional health

Remind participants of their statutory duties by making sure work is within prescribed guidelines, especially those around safeguarding and protecting children.

Show Slide 13, *The assessment framework*, which reminds us what children need to be safe and have every opportunity for their optimum mental and physical welfare.

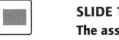

SLIDE 13
The assessment framework

61

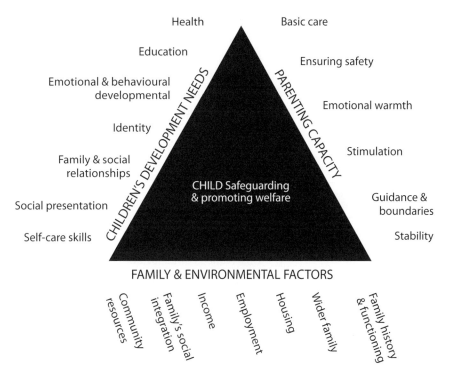

(Department of Health, 2000)

Next, we will look at how to undertake direct work with children in order to ascertain their wishes and feelings.

Gathering general information for assessment

Introduce Slides 14 and 15 to participants by explaining that these show the general information that one needs before either starting an assessment or any in-depth life history or direct work with a child.

Tell participants that becoming familiar with the information in the first five chapters of the *Handbook* and in the corresponding chapters on the *Techniques CD* will assist their overall assessment skills. They will probably find particularly helpful the lists of signs and symptoms of important indicators of abuse and medically named syndromes (such as Foetal Alcohol Syndrome) in Chapter 5.

SLIDE 14
Assessment tools

1 Core assessment
   - Flowchart: Information and chronology from case file, child and family, ethnicity, culture and religion
2 Medical information
   - Growth charts and clinical information
3 Developmental age
   - Is the child stuck?
   - The six strands of development
4 Complete statutory assessment forms if the child is in care

SLIDE 15
Assessment tools (cont)

5 Assess educational achievements and other relevant information from school
6 Observations of behaviour by child's carer
   - Diary of child's daily pattern
7 Observations of child by outsider
8 Strengths and Difficulties Questionnaire (SDQ) for parent/carer
9 Various trauma assessment tools/Child behaviour checklists

Assessment questions

Now distribute Handout 2.4 *Quick reference assessment questions* and say that this will remind participants of the questions we ask ourselves in order to do a good assessment. Then go through this with them, showing Slide 16.

SLIDE 16
Assessment

The child:
- How does the child see his or her world?
- What has been the impact of the moves and changes in his or her life?
- What developmental stage has he or she reached?
- Who is he or she attached to?
- What are the child's needs and wishes and feelings?

Next, give out Handout 2.5, *Demonstration flowchart*. Go through this flowchart with participants, saying that, when they receive a new case, they should read the file to obtain the following information, or get it from the client's family, and then fill in this chart.

The purpose of a chart like this is four-fold:

- it forms a chronology of the child's life;
- it shows the attachments they have made and to whom;
- it records the losses, moves and changes the child has experienced, which ordinary chronologies don't;
- when looking at it completed we can see the primary losses the child has suffered, which may have been overlooked and for which the child needs to grieve.

We may well need to focus on this in our assessment and direct work if the child appears to be emotionally stuck. For example, one child came to England aged three after her granny died. Granny had been her primary attachment figure since she was six months old. The child had no verbal recollection of her granny but now, at the age of 10, was stuck emotionally. No one knew why until they discovered the loss of the grandparent and the child was able to work through it in play.

It is vital that workers keep the chronology up to date because it makes life story work much easier to do and is essential for compiling a later life letter.

Now introduce Slides 17 and 18, saying that the aim of the direct work part of any assessment is to give the child an opportunity to show or tell their story without fear of others' influence, and within a context of being kept safe and having their needs met. Say that children will tell you their story – either by projecting their feelings onto characters such as toy vehicles, animals or people, or by having a sudden adverse reaction to stimuli. In this way they will show you what they believe to be facts, or their fears and fantasies, about their life.

SLIDE 17
Direct work with children

- The child will tell us through play:
    - what his/her wishes and feelings are and what he or she needs
    - how we can meet these needs, wishes and feelings

SLIDE 18
Assessment – direct work techniques

Focus our play on finding out more about the child
We are looking for his or her perception of their world:
- Facts, fantasies and fears
- What kind of relationships does he or she have...and with whom?
- Does he or she have a sense of self?
- Where is he or she stuck? Consider each of these "strands": physical, sensory, intellectual, emotional, social and moral.

After going through Slide 18, tell participants that, when doing an assessment of a child, they also need to be aware of the child's responses to stimuli, as listed below. After observing a child's play, we can confirm, or otherwise, our findings with the child's carer and if this differs, we should record both.

- Is the child more stressed by silence or a noisy environment?
- Does he react to particular textures in clothing, animals, furniture?
- Does she react to any particular smells or sprays, deodorants, perfume?
- Is fear of bathing or swimming related to water temperature or noise?
- Is the child who delays getting ready for journeys afraid of what will happen in transit? Are journeys associated with abandonment and unforeseen change?

(Cairns, 2007)

Then tell participants that the list of things to look at in an assessment continues in Slide 19.

SLIDE 19
Assessment – direct work techniques (cont)

● How does the child understand any loss or traumatic events they have experienced?
● What are their wishes and feelings?
● Does he/she have the social emotions of empathy, pride, guilt, shame and embarrassment?

---

15 minutes	**12**	**BREAK**

45 minutes   **13   PRACTICAL SESSION ON USING ASSESSMENT TECHNIQUES**

Before beginning with practical demonstrations, it would be useful if you could make the following points.

● There are many methods of assessment but the model described below comes from the principles of play therapy first described by Axline (1967), who had a non-directive approach (described in the *Handbook* in Chapter 5: *Play and communication*). It is helpful to start with a non-directive approach in a session by using toys or objects, as this allows the child to feel free to say, or tell you, what they wish to without fear that you won't approve.

● It is important to remember that as social workers or carers it is your observations and interaction within the relationship that are all-important. The techniques are clearly useful in providing background scenery or signposts with which the child can play out, or find their way into, a story to tell you what happened to them, but it is *how you relate to them* that is key. Being a good reflective listener often goes halfway to healing the worries and muddles of the children you are working with.

● By using sensory play, house play, or a life road or map, children can show you how they perceive the world. Painting, drawing or acting out a story can also act as a trigger to memory.

● When starting the assessment, it is important (as we learned in Session 1) to set up the room, start with introductions and make clear any boundaries.

● When you are with the child, notice your feelings of transference and countertransference and use these to inform your observations and reflections on what is happening between you and the child. In this way you can see how the child experiences their world and how you can help them to process it within a safe environment.

● Whilst observing and using active listening skills, remember to watch for evidence of emotions, e.g. empathy, pride, guilt, shame and embarrassment, and how the child is demonstrating these. Children who have immature emotions have all kinds of issues when trying to relate to and process the world. For example, avoidant attachment-disordered children often don't want to know anything about the past and may pretend to themselves that Mum or Dad is going to rescue them from their present placement.

● Sometimes when working with traumatised children in an assessment, it is possible to make up a story that naturally follows on from a sand picture or a story the child has created, and this can help the child to heal and find meaning in a loss. The fact that you have "heard" the child can empower the child to find a solution to meet their needs without your ever having to be explicit about what is going on. For example, Kate and her social worker often played with the "feelings bag", together making up stories with the objects. The social worker only used objects that provided scenery, not a story line. One day Kate said she had made her own feelings bag, and as she pulled out the objects she said, 'I was hit with this strap!' 'How terrible,' said the worker, acknowledging the enormity of what the child experienced. 'What I need is this,' said Kate, handing the social worker a baby's bottle as she sat on her worker's knee, wanting to be fed. The worker got her foster carer, who then fed Kate like a baby. As you get experienced at doing this sort of work, both your own creativity and that of the child will take off and you will be surprised how easy it is to talk to them about all kinds of issues.

- As a worker you will have limited time in an assessment, so one way of saving time is to be specific by saying to the child, 'We can play one of your games, then one of mine, and finish with one of yours'. In this way the child can choose free play if they want, which is also useful because you can use this to observe what they are doing.
- Explain that it is essential that participants acknowledge appropriately any strong feelings the child shows – they may be the first person to hear what the child is saying. If you shut down a child by telling them off for some aspect of their behaviour, this may make it impossible for the child to share this information ever again. It's therefore important that you try to stay with what they are telling you and really concentrate, even if you don't like what you are hearing. Avoid moving on to solving the problem; try to feel their pain with them.
- Sometimes giving the child a break outside in the middle of a session is all you need to release tension – for example, going out for a short game of football can help to release such tension.

Answering children's questions and finding out about their experiences

Explain that certain techniques can be useful in answering specific questions children ask, or in eliciting information about their experiences, as described below.

Answering the question 'Why am I here?' (i.e. not at home)

- Give out Handouts 2.6 and 2.7 with the two stories, *The river of happy and sad and lonely feelings* and *The seed story*.
- Go through the stories as per the instructions on the handouts, explaining how participants can use these. Tell participants that they need to explain to the child why he or she is having this assessment and why they are staying with foster carers, and why you are coming to find out what their wishes and feelings are.
- Invite and answer any questions from participants.

Getting children to describe happy and traumatic experiences

- Distribute Handout 2.8, *Cartoon pictures with instruction sheet.*
- Ask participants to look at a specific cartoon drawing and discuss how they could use this with children.
- Explain that this technique is very good for helping the child to describe happy and traumatic events. Suggest that participants look at Margot Sunderland's book *Draw on your Emotions* (1998) for further techniques.

Assessing sibling relationships

Remind participants about the use of puppets or a telephone, as third objects between you and the child (as described in Session 1). Draw their attention also to masks and fuzzy felts as described in Chapter 5: *Play and communication* on the *Techniques CD*. These are good for assessing sibling relationships – see the instructions there on how to use these.

Assessing how in touch with their feelings a child is

- Distribute Handout 2.9, *Feelings faces*. Show how you might use these with a child's drawings or with the stories by asking the child to choose a feeling face to describe an aspect of their picture or story.
- Explain that, in order to establish how in touch a child is with their feelings and senses, a worker/carer could start an assessment session with some free play, or a sensory bag game or silly senses game (as described on the *Techniques CD*, in *Assessing needs, wishes and feelings*).
- Remind participants that they could also use paper eco maps, as described in Session 1, and sand trays.

Using sand trays to raise themes

Sand trays are really useful because the child can construct a whole world in them, with "above the surface" and "below the surface" stories portrayed. The sand acts as a sensory stimulus to unconscious memories held in the mid-brain and limbic system and in this way the child is able to tap into fears and old worries, such as not having enough food or about violence.

- Tell participants that doing a sand tray with a child in a session can help find out who the members of their family are. But once you have this information, you might want to know how the child feels about their family. Say that the *Going on a journey* (see Game No. 43 on the *Techniques CD*, Chapter 6) is a useful one that can follow on from a session using the sand tray, and can be useful in confirming things learned in the sand tray session.
- Explain that, to work on this story with a child, they would need to have a flipchart sheet or toy bus (which you would probably have if you are working in a toy room). The adult would start by drawing a bus on the flipchart, or showing the child a toy bus and various figures that can be put in it. They would then do the following.
  - Ask the child to pretend they are going on holiday with their family and that they are going there by bus.
  - Then ask the child whom they would sit next to on the bus. The child should then draw those people in the bus, or put the figures inside it.
  - You could ask the child if they would like their holiday to be in a caravan, a tent, a hotel or a castle.
  - They should then draw the tents, caravan, etc., and say to the child that each room or tent has only two beds in it.
  - Ask the child who on the bus they would feel comfortable sharing their tent or room with. This can trigger disclosures or indicate trauma. Use sensitive reflective listening if a child does make a disclosure.
  - End by chatting about the rest of the family or let the child play out further scenarios and just reflect back the feelings he or she seems to be expressing.

Explain to participants that the stories of maltreated children mostly end in disaster, showing no means of conflict resolution. These children tend to use magical thinking to go from disaster to having a wonderful time with the abusing adult. They also often regress in play to the level when they lost the primary care-giver or show in their play that they have missed many developmental milestones, i.e. preferring to play peek-a-boo games in the sand where a typical child of that age would not want to play in the sand. They might also show a desperate need for food and nurture by returning to making food with play dough and being unable to share it with dolls or puppets, or they may just shut down completely.

Next, show participants Slides 20, 21 and 22 of the sand tray stories and read out the relevant Notes relating to each one. This explains how sand trays can be used as a means of revealing themes in a child's thoughts and experiences. These are also available as Handout 2.10.

SLIDE 20

SLIDE 21

SLIDE 22

Starting off a story that a child can complete

Tell participants that the purpose of the following ideas is to help them discover how a child sees and experiences the world and whether there is any evidence of risk in their situation. Also, as stated before, these ideas can help you to learn what the child's wishes and feelings are in order to assist in your overall assessment.

The technique requires the adult to start off a story. The child is then invited to continue the narrative, with a few prompts from the adult, and say what happens next.

These are called "story stems" and are used in assessment to help the child tell you what is happening, and can be used to assess the child's attachment and internal working model. People need to be formally trained to use story stems (details are given in Chapters 8 and 9 of the *Handbook*).

Now ask participants to turn to the printout they have of the *Techniques CD*, and point out the special toy and resources lists and Chapter 5: *Assessment*, which contains a list of useful ideas.

You could then also demonstrate to participants how to use the *Bears* cards, if you have a set. These are designed to enable children to describe feelings and difficult events in life. The pack contains a useful booklet on how to use the cards, and the dialogue you might use to ascertain a child's wishes and feelings.

Also, if you have a set, show participants the Barnardo's *All about me* game. This is designed to help a child talk about events and feelings they have experienced. This game is very effective in helping explore whether children feel safe and can also show how they feel about themselves in relation to others.

Explain to participants that you can also use dolls' house play as part of an assessment to get them to start talking about their family and what's happening in it. Or you can start off a story by saying, 'Once upon a time, this little child (or animal)...' and then ask the child to continue the story as in story stem work, but in this way just giving the child an opportunity to play. If you use reflective listening during this, the child will often describe happy and difficult times within their environment or home.

You can also use the "feelings bag" collection described in Session 1 to start off a story. To use this, do the following:

- Say to the child, '*You* choose three objects from the bag and I will do the same'. When you as the worker choose objects, only choose those that create a sense of place, sound, or a home setting – as illustrated in the next bullet point. (In this way your part of the story will not lead the child.)
- For example, you could start off a story like this: 'Once upon a time there was a forest...' (at this point you could put up a couple of trees). Then invite the child to add an object, with you then adding another, and so on. This enables children to start to use metaphor as a medium for sharing worries. You can verify this by saying, 'If any of these objects were in your family, which object would you choose to be whom?'

Also point out the "Day in the life" idea (Game No. 56) on the *Techniques CD*.

Working with reluctant children

Now go on to briefly explain to participants the following ideas, which are useful for working with children unwilling or hesitant to participate.

- *Drawings:* see the *Techniques CD*, in *Play and communication*. These can be started as a way to work with reluctant children and involve the adult drawing a picture of simple scenery such as a road or hills, sun and clouds, etc. The child is then invited to add to the picture with their own drawings, including those of people, or they can be asked to place animals or people onto the paper scenery. Then invite the child to tell you about their picture.
- *Favourite things game:* see Game No. 34 on the *Techniques CD*. Cut out pictures from magazines, e.g. food, clothes, pop stars, bands, sports or animals, etc. Use these to talk about the child's likes and dislikes. Observe facts, feelings and fantasies by talking about how they might do these things in reality: do they play an instrument or is this just a wish list? Or what might *prevent* them from doing these things?
- Remind participants about the scribble drawings, covered this morning, which can also be useful as a tool with reluctant children.

Window exercise: finding out what is blocking a child's progress

The purpose of this exercise is to help the child look at the past in relation to the present and see what specific fear might be blocking their progress, and stopping them from moving forward. You might have used something similar in your own experience. See instructions under Game No. 53 on the *Techniques CD*, *Assessing needs, wishes and feelings*. Distribute Handout 2.11.

- Give participants paper and pens and ask them to draw a window with four panes.
- Ask participants to complete their own window picture following the instructions on the handout.
- They should then find a partner and listen to each other in a reflective way.

- Remind participants only to share what they feel comfortable sharing.
- Say that they can use puppets or animals that they brought with them, so that they can practise using a third object as a listener. (The purpose of the third object here is so that the child can talk only to the puppet rather than the worker if they don't want eye contact.)
- Ask for comments from the group about how it felt using this technique.

15 minutes   **14**

EXERCISES: ASSESSING PARENTING STYLES AND IDENTIFYING CHILDREN'S ATTACHMENT FIGURES

Depending on the needs of participants (as explained below), use one of the following exercises with them.

Explain that you will now show them an experiential exercise that they can use with children. The point here is to experience for themselves what the exercise feels like.

- *Parental messages:* This technique should only be used if you are teaching social workers, or workers who are dealing with adolescents who are preparing to leave care. It is also useful as an assessment tool when assessing prospective adoptive parents to obtain an individual's parenting history. Give out a copy of Handout 2.12, *Parent message cards and instructions,* to each participant, with instructions for this as given at the bottom of the handout.
- *The magic carpet ride* (Game No. 48): Instructions for doing this can be found on the *Techniques CD*, Chapter 6: *Assessing needs, wishes and feelings.* This can be used by a multidisciplinary group – for example, one containing social workers, foster carers, assessment workers in assessment centres, etc.

Parental messages

Explain that this idea comes from the *In Touch with Parents* BAAF course of 1985 (no longer in print). It is a good method for helping children to express how they perceived their parents'/carers' basic messages or behaviour towards them, and helps you to talk to the child about the way in which these messages were given. This can also help children to understand why they might need *new* parents.

- Start by asking participants to look through the messages on Handout 2.12, *Parent message cards,* and to choose 10 that they think they received from their parents, whether positive or negative.
- They should then choose (from those 10) two messages they feel comfortable sharing with a listening partner.
- Ask them to start to share, adding that they might like to say how that message was conveyed to them. (Remind them only to share what they feel comfortable sharing, as this exercise is not a therapy session!)
- Then ask them to choose one message that they would most like to pass on to their own children.
- Then, in a group feedback session, ask them to share which messages they would pass on to their children or the children in their care.
- End by demonstrating how participants could use this technique in their work with children and young people, i.e. in assessments of different types of parent – birth/adoptive/foster. (Say that children's guardians could also use this to help in arbitration cases.)

- Suggest that participants could keep the parent message sheets and photocopy them for use or cover them in sticky-backed plastic. They could also make some clean blanks so parents or children can write their own messages on these if the ones provided don't reflect their views.

The magic carpet ride

The purpose of this exercise is to find out who a child's primary attachment figure is. It is a good exercise if you are worried about using the parent message game with your group of participants. The game works well if participants are relaxed so make sure that you tell the story quietly. (The exercise originally comes from Violet Oaklander's *Windows to our Children* and has been adapted by the authors.) Doing the exercise will also give participants confidence in using these techniques themselves.

- Give participants pen and paper and say to them, 'I want to tell a story'.
- Read to participants the instructions for The Magic Carpet Ride, Game No. 48 on the *Techniques CD*.
- When you have finished, ask the participants to draw what they imagined in their mind as they listened. As you are working with adults in a big group, some may not actually have "seen" anything because they may not be feeling particularly relaxed, but don't worry if this is the case. Those who *didn't* see anything will just sit quietly or draw anything they like. At the end, tell them this does not matter to children: if they enjoy this type of game, they will get into it.
- When participants have finished drawing, ask the group as a whole if anyone saw and then drew someone. Ask if anyone would feel able to share who they saw with the group. Explain that often the person they "saw" is likely to be the person to whom they feel most attached and whom they feel safe to be with (it could be a granny, mother, father, husband or sibling). Explain that children will only be able to do this activity if they have become sufficiently relaxed and you have established a minimum of trust with them. The child would also have had to have an attachment figure they once felt safe with.

Explain that children can often carry out this exercise as they tend to be less inhibited than adults but, even so, not every technique works with all children and so we need to be flexible. Explain that it's a good idea to be familiar with several games so that (for reasons explained earlier) you can say to a child: 'Would you like to play one of your games and then one of mine?'

Explain that the Loving and caring water game (Game No. 81 on the *Techniques CD*) is also effective to use for:

- observing whom the child feels most attached to;
- helping the child understand and find meaning for losses; and
- starting the healing process.

Say that you will be demonstrating this game in Session 3.

10 minutes   **15**   **SUMMARISING ASSESSMENTS IN REPORTS**

Explain that what you are looking for in total in this kind of direct work assessment is summarised in the three final slides. Then show Slides 23–25, reminding participants that they already saw Slide 23 just after lunch.

As you go through the slides, amplify their content by referring to the Notes.

SLIDE 23
Direct work assessment

- Look for themes and patterns of how the child sees their world, and how they express their wishes and feelings.
- Notice how they make relationships and the nature of these.
- Are there any developmental delays?
- What is their experience of trauma and loss?

For each of the above, you need three pieces of evidence from your direct work.

SLIDE 24
Assessment result...

1. Developmental age of the child
   Where the child is stuck (if he or she is!)
2. Intellectual stage
3. Social behaviour
4. Attachments

To anyone?
To whom?
What sort of attachments?

SLIDE 25
...Assessment result

5. Who could give permission for the child to move or change?
6. What does a child with this profile need?

Summary:
What is in the best interests of the child?

Passing on information about assessment to others

Explain to participants that it is essential to tell a child what you are going to say to the judge at the court hearing and the team, and your reasons for doing this. For example, you could say something like:

- 'I told the judge that you told me that you loved them lots but you told me you were scared.' (As the adult, it's important to remove the responsibility for the decision from the child.) 'I told him I didn't think it was safe for you to stay with Mum and Dad because they really couldn't remember not to fight or remember to feed you or keep you safe all of the time.'
- Or, 'Unfortunately Mum/Dad couldn't keep you safe and Dad had to go to a "time out place" called prison because he couldn't keep the rules.'
- Or 'Mum's drinking problem made her mind so muddled she forgot to make dinner or take you to school.'

Always be honest with the child. Paraphrase back to the child what he or she has told you and let them know what you will be saying to the guardian/judge. Say that you *will* tell the court what their wishes and feelings are but that you may not be able to agree with what he/she hopes for, and why. In our experience, the child is usually very relieved about this. Nonetheless, the child will still be experiencing the pain of loss and will need your help to come to terms with this.

After the court hearing, tell the child what was agreed in simple and easy-to-understand words that are age appropriate, and tell them what the outcome means for them. If they can't seem to take in this information, try using a story that will act as a metaphor to ease the pain.

Honesty is always reassuring for children because they often know deep down what is right but have such loyalty to their parents that they cannot say so.

One child said, 'I am glad you told the court what you thought, not what I thought I wanted. I was really cross with you at the time but I couldn't tell you that Mum was never there, I am glad you noticed.'

If you need further resources and ideas, look on the *Techniques CD* under play equipment. Computer games are particularly useful with adolescents but this a changing market. Try to find up-to-date products using the search engines of NCH.

5 minutes

16   CLOSING THE SESSION

Ask participants whether they have any final questions. Then remind them of the date when they will return for the next session. Say that in the next session we will be working on identity issues, life histories and moving children between home situations in a way that avoids trauma and helps them reattach.

Suggest that participants find some time between this session and the next to try doing some reflective listening with children using a puppet.

SESSION 3
Building a positive self-esteem and starting a life history journey

OVERVIEW

	Section	Timing
1	Welcome and ball exercise	**20 minutes**
2	Goals for Session 3	**20 minutes**
3	Exercise: *Case study on Ryan*	**45 minutes**
4	Break	**15 minutes**
5	Presentation: *Building identity and self-esteem*	**15 minutes**
6	Introduction to direct work methods	**30 minutes**
7	Demonstration of the water game	**15 minutes**
8	Exercise: *The hand-drawing game*	**15 minutes**
9	Self-esteem building techniques	**10 minutes**
10	Exercise: *Family tree*	**15 minutes**
11	Talking about difference and heritage	**10 minutes**
12	Demonstration of the counters game	**5 minutes**
13	Lunch	**1 hour**
14	Introduction to life history work	**15 minutes**
15	Exercise: *The orange game*	**20 minutes**
16	Exercise: *The "first memory" game*	**25 minutes**
17	Thinking about how to record information in life history work	**15 minutes**
18	Break	**15 minutes**
19	Demonstration of methods and techniques for life story work	**20 minutes**
20	Exercise: *Fears about doing direct work*	**20 minutes**
21	Final points	**10 minutes**
22	Closing the session	**5 minutes**

PREPARATION

In preparation for the next two sessions of the course (Sessions 3 and 4), read Chapter 7, *Helping children in transition*, in the *Handbook* up to the end of the book and also the chapter of the same name on the *Techniques CD* up to the end of the CD. This will familiarise you with the suggestions and work to be covered in the next two sessions.

PARTICULAR RESOURCES NEEDED FOR THIS SESSION

- A soft ball that can be thrown between members of the group
- A black plastic binbag filled with various memory-provoking items, to be used as a visual aid
- For the demonstration of the water game, a plastic bowl, plastic cups, two jugs, cling-film and a towel
- For the counters game, some counters or beans or tiddlywinks and a cup
- For the orange game, enough oranges and paper towels for each participants to have one
- Small dolls' house, furniture and a couple of toy cars
- For the discussion and demonstration on identity and life story work, it is useful to have the following:
  - a small photo album, either empty or containing photos
  - some dual heritage dolls of Playmobil size
  - a small toy car
  - an address book that has not yet been filled in
  - a photo of a memorabilia box
  - a pre-prepared demonstration A4-size life story folder to show how you might use headings and divide identity work from life history work (see Chapter 7: *Helping children in transition* in the *Handbook*). On each page of the folder use the headings and question lists to be found under *Transition* on the *Techniques CD*.
  - you could also use some of the BAAF books about memories and life story work to assist this demonstration. These are listed in the book list on www.baaf.org.uk
  - there is also a very useful book called *Life Story Books for Adopted Children* by Joy Rees (2009)
  - either a photo of the canvas life story map (Game No. 61, described on the *Techniques CD*), or one that you have made yourself using paper or canvas, on which you can demonstrate how to use such a map with miniature furniture and dolls as visual aids

HANDOUTS

- 3.1 *Session 3: Overview*
- 3.2 *Case study on Ryan*
- Copies for each participant of Session 3's PowerPoint presentation.

20 minutes

1   WELCOME AND BALL EXERCISE

Display Slide 1, showing the title of the session's course.

SLIDE 1

Building a positive self-esteem and starting a life history journey

Welcome everyone back again and say that you will be starting today with a short exercise that is aimed at reminding everyone of each other's names.

Ball exercise

This exercise is intended to bring the group back together again.

Ask participants to stand in a circle and then get them to throw a ball around the group, calling out their name every time they catch it. Do this for five minutes.

Course reminders

After the game is over, start by summarising the learning from Sessions 1 and 2, making the points listed below.

- Session 1: Tell participants that, in order to understand what followed in subsequent sessions, we started by looking at children's development, as you need to know at what developmental stage children do things. We also looked at how relationships, attachment, trauma and loss affect the way we build a sense of self, self-esteem and a feeling of being unique yet belonging to a group. We also began to practise listening skills using a third object.
- Session 2: We discussed separation and loss, managing difficult behaviour and starting direct work assessment, as well as learning some helpful techniques to help children process their loss and manage powerful feelings.

Remind participants of:

- the comfort breaks and safety rules and when to expect meal breaks;
- confidentiality rules.

Say that, as this course is necessarily experiential and will be thought provoking for all involved, it may well cause some participants to need to speak to the trainer privately if they are finding something difficult emotionally. Let them know when you would be available for this. Tell participants that they should also monitor how they are feeling about material presented and that, if they start to feel overwhelmed or strongly affected by a particular issue, they can choose to sit out of an exercise.

Point out where you have placed copies of useful books to look at.

Give out the overview for the session – Handout 3.1.

Finally, ask participants to please turn off their mobile phones/other devices.

Invite feedback

Ask participants whether they tried out any of the techniques they learnt from the first two sessions of the course, such as using a third object with a child, and ask what the results were. Invite participants briefly to share their experiences of doing so, as this can give others confidence to try out things for themselves.

If the technique used didn't quite go to plan, explain that they need not be worried because allowing a child the space to follow their need with your listening support, within your trusting relationship with them, is what is required for healing – not the following of the exact instructions.

Explain that today's programme will be conducted using the same experiential workshop style used in Sessions 1 and 2.

20 minutes   **2   GOALS FOR SESSION 3**

Show Slide 2 and go through the goals of the session with participants.

SLIDE 2
Goals for Session 3

- To understand the tasks in transition
    - Identity, life story, moving on
- How to help the child by using a third object to answer the following questions:
    - Who am I?
    - Where do I belong?
    - Where am I going?

Identity: Who am I?

Introducing the black plastic binbag

Tell participants that we will now be looking at the black plastic binbag, the purpose of which is to use its symbolic contents to illustrate what we don't know about the child and what is often hidden about them before you take the trouble to find it out. This hidden information is the reason why we do direct work, with the aim of helping the child process their story.

Now show Slide 3.

SLIDE 3
Who am I?

Object passed from here to there	Skills
Sensory experiences	Friendships
A bundle of feelings	Treasures, my very own
I have memories of places in me	Sex (experience? abuse?)
Fantasies, hopes and illusions	Religion, ethnicity and culture
Secrets	What really happened, and is happening
Mum, Dad and siblings	

After you have shown Slide 3, produce the black plastic binbag you have prepared in advance (following the instructions below). Explain to participants that you will now think about the question "Who am I?"

Say that children often come into care with their belongings stuffed into a bag like this and say of the bag, 'Oh, it's just rubbish.' We often know very little about a child coming into care for the first time. This bag represents the unknown child we don't know, and about whom we can find out by discovering what the objects in the bag represent for them. Sensory objects, like the examples described below, trigger all sorts of thoughts and feelings and are very helpful in the healing process for building identity and doing life history work.

Say that the contents of this bag are symbols that could represent a child's hopes, dreams, fears and special memories. Now take each object out of the bag and talk about what they might mean for a child, or what else these things might symbolise.

For example:

- *A party dress:* this might represent a party they have fond memories of.
- *An Afro hair comb:* this might represent parental care, how the child was groomed – which might have been the only way a parent showed care.
- *A perfume bottle:* this might represent a smell they liked or remind them of other smells they didn't like, e.g. tobacco smoke, which their house always smelt of.
- *A toy such as a yellow lorry:* this might have been what they told their troubles to under the table whilst hiding from their parents as the parents fought with each other.
- *A little family of Playmobil people:* this might represent people in their family, including a range of relatives.
- *A red cloth under which there is a purple cloth* (pull red cloth out with a flourish): this can be used to demonstrate how emotions can mask other emotions, e.g. depression can hide anger, anger can hide sadness.
- *A picture of their favourite food:* this might represent a child's need for nurture or a memory of a special dish or a way to be in touch with their particular cultural background.
- *A cuddly bear and baby bottle:* these might represent the hugs and baby-nurturing the child might have needed but did not receive.
- *An 'I am a Hindu' book or similar:* this might represent the child's religious background.
- Finally, a *little box containing a couple of things that represent a child's secrets:* you could take out a ribbon or a stone and say you don't know what they represent for the child but they will let you know through their play.

Belongings like those in such a bag are often potent symbols of what the child is bringing into care in terms of their feelings and emotions. When you ask a child directly about their wishes and feelings, they often can't make connections. What they bring with them can represent feelings and thoughts inside them. In your reflections on these, you can help them understand these remains and mementos of their earlier life, which can be very helpful in the healing process of building identity and doing life history work. So it is very important that carers keep what might appear to be "rubbish" in order to jog the memory for life history work.

As you finish, say to participants that as well as this bag showing the type of things a child might bring, many children feel as if they are an object passed from here to there, losing bits of themselves on the way. (This is a particular problem for asylum-seeking children trying to get used to a new language as well as a culture.) One child described poignantly how this felt, by saying:

'I am a parcel that never got properly unwrapped in any place and this mummy and daddy don't know who I am either.'

This child had made, from a square of clay, a parcel with a tiny face peeking out of the corner.

Preparation for identity and life history work

Show Slide 4, which lists what needs to be gathered by way of basic preparation by the worker before doing identity and life history direct work with a child, using the Notes to amplify points made.

SLIDE 4
Preparation to do types of transition work

- Complete assessment of children's needs, wishes and feelings
- Find out if children know why they are living in care or having help from you
- Gather facts from files and, if possible, interview parents or past carers
- Make a timeline, adding the impact of any changes recorded
- Think about hierarchy of attachments and who else children are missing
- Give the child a sense of hope by showing your commitment to their process by setting out clearly how many times you are coming and when
- Make sure their skills are being enhanced by carers

Other things to think about when planning your work

Take participants through the following points.

- For social workers, all statutory visits are an opportunity for direct work, starting by listening reflectively to the child's grief. During the period when plans for the child's future are still undecided, you should support the child's carer to do the same, as well as encouraging the building of a child's self-esteem by developing his or her basic skills and talents (see in the *Handbook*, Chapter 7: *Helping children in transition*, pp 80–1).

- Direct work in transition needs good preparation, following assessment of the child, as discussed in Session 2. You need to consider the time you have available and the number of direct work sessions you are able to commit to, as well as the child's timescale before being placed permanently.

- Think about what the child needs during this uncertain time and before the court case. Remember Session 2's framework, which covered what a worker should do and when, i.e. an assessment of the child's needs and the type of transitional support, grief work, identity work, life orientation map, life history work, moving on. Also see the *Handbook*, Chapter 7: *Helping children in transition*, which explains in detail how to structure your work.

- Tell participants that we need to start with good preparation, and so collecting and checking facts of the child's history are essential. Remember to use the flowcharts given in Session 2 to collect facts. If the child is already in a foster family or a permanent placement (i.e. if any participant is an adopter, long-term foster carer or kinship carer), the carer needs to make sure to collect relevant medical, health and life history facts from their social worker. Always check any documents, such as copies of birth certificates you have, for dates and names before showing them to a child or young person. It can cause great distress if a child believes they were born on one date, but their birth certificate says something different, or if their dad hasn't got the same name as the one they expected.

- In preparation: Tell participants that they should decide who is going to be doing what task in the team that surrounds the child and tell them where they will find the necessary information (see the *Handbook*, Chapter 7: *Helping children in transition*, pp 83–87) on the roles people could take to share the work.

- During this uncertain time, start any life history work and/or book with the identity aspect, i.e. "Who am I?" Orientate the child in their story by using a life orientation map (see No. 58 on *Techniques CD*). Do not attempt to do in-depth life history work at this time as the child will be unable to process it because they will be shocked and anxious about what is happening to them. Although you will be unable to answer vital questions about what is happening to the child, you can listen reflectively, making no promises and doing normal activities with them. For example, if they ask, 'How long am I staying with you?' see the toilet-roll game, No. 1 on the *Techniques CD*.

- If the court decides that the child should return home to their birth parents, he or she should have been given a photo album that was created by the foster carer of the things they did while they were away, as well as being helped to devise a story about what they did when they were away (which could be in metaphor, e.g. 'The little rabbit had to stay in another burrow...'). This helps with re-attachment when children are confused about why they could not be with their parents for a period of time. Sharing a child's experiences breaks down the fear and anxiety between birth parents and child and helps them pick up the pieces more easily. This practice is especially important for babies, as they grow so quickly. It helps if the foster carer can prepare an album in which important milestones are recorded so that the birth parent doesn't miss out on any "first steps" that occurred while the child was not in their care.

- If the child is to stay in the care system, and long-term plans have been agreed, this is when we can start "repair life history work" with the child.

45 minutes   **3**   ██ **EXERCISE: CASE STUDY ON RYAN** ██

Explain to participants that they are now going to do an exercise about a boy called Ryan, who has had an assessment. In their groups they are going to think about:

- what sense they make of what has been found out about Ryan, as described in the case study, and
- how in practice one would help Ryan understand what you have learnt about his needs and his history.

Give out a copy of Handout 3.2 *Case study on Ryan* to each participant. Ask them to read the case study, and when they have finished doing so, show them Slides 5, 6 and 7; Slide 6 is a prompt to remind participants of what a child needs to be in touch with before he can process information and Slide 7 contains some questions.

Tell participants to get into small groups and give them some sheets of flipchart paper and pens to write their answers. As the participants in your group may come from a range of disciplines, it can be quite helpful to mix up the groups so they can bring different perspectives to the exercise. This will also make it easier for them to understand the difference in their roles and to think about how they might work together as a team around the child.

SLIDE 5
Identity: Who am I?

Who am I?
How do I feel about myself?
Am I in touch with my feelings?
Do I have words for feelings?

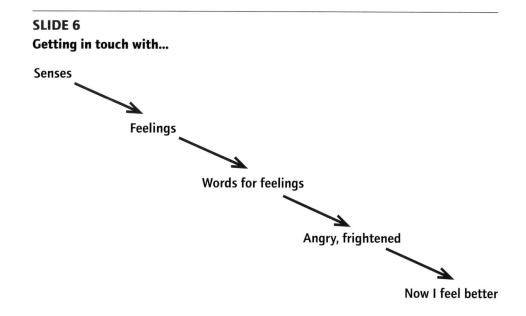

SLIDE 6
Getting in touch with...

Senses

Feelings

Words for feelings

Angry, frightened

Now I feel better

SLIDE 7
Exercise on Ryan

- Whom is he attached to?
- What type of attachment do you think he has?
- How many losses has he had?
- How would you build his self-esteem?
- What work needs to be done? Who would do which parts of the work?
- Make lists of needs and practical intervention
- What other information do you need to help him build his identity and to make a life history book?

Feedback from exercise

Spend 15 minutes collecting the feedback from the groups and then display their sheets of flipchart paper on the wall. These will relate, and add, to your presentation and discussion after the break. This will also help participants to own what they already know.

For your information, the Notes accompanying Slide 7 contain the answers to the questions asked. If the group has not supplied these in their feedback, make sure they are clear about these points.

| *15 minutes* | **4** | **BREAK** |

| *15 minutes* | **5** | **PRESENTATION: BUILDING IDENTITY AND SELF-ESTEEM** |

Make a presentation using the points below and, if you wish, adding material from pp 79–92 in Chapter 7 of the *Handbook*, headed *Identity* and *Developing a personal narrative*. Use Slides 8 and 9 as illustrations.

Start by saying to participants that throughout our lives we ask ourselves, 'Who am I?' and at each stage we arrive at a different answer (Cole, 1996, p. 402).

At this stage of identity-building we aim to:

- help the child to become aware of his/her own senses and bodily feelings, by using sensory material to encourage him/her to experience these feelings and then find words to describe them;
- orient them to the changes in their lives (i.e paper life map) – rehearsal helps children to manage change;
- encourage them to build their skills, so they gain competence and resilience, recover from their losses and develop more positive feelings about themselves.

Put up Slide 8, *The self*, which they first saw in Session 1.

SLIDE 8
The self

- 0–2 months   Emerging self
- 2/3–7/9 months   Core self
- 9–18 months   Subjective self
- 2 years   Verbal self
- Beyond   Narrative self

(Stern, 1985)

Developing a personal narrative

Tell participants the following:

- A child's brain is like a computer that can work only if it has been properly programmed to make the necessary neural connections. In the early years the parents are the programmers of their children's brains.
- The child must have separated psychologically from their birth mother in order to gain a sense of self, usually in conjunction with attaining language.
- A personal narrative gives us a personal theory of who we are, both to ourselves and to others.
- As our horizons expand beyond the family, we alter our perception of the world. So, by telling and processing our story, we can alter the outcome of our lives and thus gain a better sense of self. In this way, our view of ourselves can change from the role we may have been given by the family script to a more accurate one.

Safeguarding children within the care system requires giving the children with whom we work what Hughes refers to as an "integrated self" – a secure, balanced sense of self and identity. When children have been repeatedly threatened and traumatised, their "self" becomes fragmented (Hughes, 2000).

Show participants Slide 9 and explain it using the Notes provided.

SLIDE 9
Building of self

Safety	Threat
● *Integrated self*	● *Fragmented self*
– *Resonating affect*	– *Reactive affect*
– *Flexible behaviour*	– *Impulsive behaviour*
– *Reflective thought*	– *Rigid thought*
– *Coherent narrative*	– *Disorganised narrative*
– *Presence*	– *Dissociation*

(Hughes, 2000)

You could end the presentation by looking at the signs of low self-esteem in children, which are listed on p. 82 in Chapter 7: *Helping children in transition* in the *Handbook*. Remind participants that these signs can often present as part of the stages in loss, so listening to a child's grief can in fact also be part of the cure for low self-esteem.

Helping a child build a sense of self

Tell participants that in the next section you will be looking at what is needed to help a child build a sense of self, change how he sees and feels about his body, gain a more positive narrative about himself, and show how to record it in the life history book.

Show participants Slide 10.

SLIDE 10
Support in transition

Through his senses he begins to express:
grief, shock, anger and denial...
... about the loss or change in his life.
We help to give him a stronger sense of self, through development of his skills.
We can then move on to orientate him in his life.

30 minutes

6 INTRODUCTION TO DIRECT WORK METHODS

Now tell participants that you will be once again looking at how to start direct work, which they began learning about in Sessions 1 and 2. Remind them that the aim of this work is to empower the child to recover from losses by exploring the muddles of his or her earlier life in relation to his or her understanding about the here and now. In this way, the child will be able to sort out misperceptions, grieve and build a more secure sense of identity.

Go through Slides 11, 12 and 13, and as you do this, refer back to the case study about Ryan and the answers participants gave to the questions, in order to validate what they said and to add anything that might be missing.

SLIDE 11
Starting direct work

Start with where the child is
- Who am I?
  Give the child a sense of self – his place in the family, ethnic group, culture, religion, his skills, likes or dislikes, feelings and senses

SLIDE 12
Identity

Stuck children:
- Have they had a loss or change?
- What kind of attachment do they have? And with whom?
- Have they grieved for the lost person, place, pet or thing?
- Are they confused about their ethnicity, religion or culture?
- Do they know who is in their family?
- Do they know where they live?

SLIDE 13
Starting a session with a child

- Go through basic safety rules, boundaries, time limits of session and confidentiality and child protection issues
- Discuss with the child the number of times you will be working with them
- Promise only what you can deliver – make it clear if you can only offer a few sessions at a time
- All children will be somewhere in the "six stages of grief" and may regress
- Children need time to process grief and to get used to new information
- Give the child a folder for their pictures and a memory box

Explain to participants that we start life history work and making life story books by building the child's "identity", and recording this as the first part of the life story book. In this way we ground the child in the present before going back over the past.

Show and pass round to participants the identity and life story folder you have created. Or show any BAAF books on life story work, or Joy Rees' book, *Life Story Books for Adopted Children* (Jessica Kingsley Publishers, 2009).

Explain to participants how one can make a "memory chest" for a child. For example, you could use a plastic chest of drawers that can be found in a DIY shop – see No. 64 on the *Techniques CD* for instructions. Explain that the child can use the different drawers to keep the treasures, trinkets and belongings they came into care with, as well as his or her life history books, school paintings and other mementos. This can then accompany the child from the foster home to their permanent substitute home, giving the clear message that the child's history is important and not to be put away.

As you work through the "identity" part of the child's life history, using metaphors, stories and storyboard pictures, help the child choose a ring binder that has light cardboard and plastic sleeves in it. Suggest they might like to place a photo of themselves on the front page with their date of birth and present age. Suggest they might like to prepare a collage of their favourite things to do and eat (you can use the list of ideas in No. 34 on the *Techniques CD*). In this they can keep the photos, drawings, and recorded facts, fears and fantasies about themselves that emerge as you work through the life events that are part of their story. Most children don't like to do the actual recording but will decorate the page or add pictures, take photos and practise the techniques suggested to build self-esteem.

How to start the work involved in building self-esteem and repairing a child's damaging life experiences

Explain to participants that, when preparing to work with a child on creating their identity/ life history work, it's important to go through the following stages.

- The first step is to agree who will be in the team around the child, and work together to assign roles – who will be responsible for what. For example:
    - building skills and making the identity part of the book could be done by the foster carer
    - making the life history part of the book and taking the child on visits to old schools, etc, could be the social worker's task or the foster carer's, but if it is the carer then the social worker should provide them with comprehensive facts and be involved to give support. (In some cases, life story books are given to administrative staff to make, but this should only happen in conjunction with the sessions the social worker has with the child to help the child process their history; otherwise the child will not feel that they own their story.)
- Next, think about who is going to organise future meetings and how much time can be given by everyone to do the task. Consider who is going to motivate everyone to do their part. Many people feel there is just not enough time to do this work. However, it is quite possible to do it during the statutory six-weekly visits if you plan it and do a small piece at a time. From the time the child comes into care, collect photos and drawings the child has made with you (take a photo of them as these often last better) and add them to the book or memorabilia. This is why it really helps to divide up the tasks, especially collating the final book. The social worker can then go over the book or final product with the child, adding in what the child says as a result of all the work. This helps the child to take a fresh look at their life and process it. Refer participants to p. 83 of Chapter 7 in the *Handbook* where the role of the social worker is considered and to p. 84 on the role of parents and carers.
- Ask relatives of the child to collect together information and memorabilia as an *aide mémoire*, or use things the child brought with them from previous placements.

Gaining the child's trust

Now tell participants that, when working with a child, you would do the following in order to build trust between you. Also, this will show that you are committed to the child getting the answers he/she needs and to understanding who they are and why they came into care.

- Offer blocks of six sessions at a time.
- When working through the 'Who am I?' part of the process, make sure you use listening skills and session techniques – see setting up a session in Appendix 1 p. 144 in the *Handbook*.
- Remember to use PACE when working with the child: playful, acceptance, curiosity and empathy.

Answering the question "Why did I come here?"

This is a question that comes up repeatedly when a child is in a new family.

- Say to participants that, when faced with this question, it is useful to remind the child of the illustrations that appear on Handouts 2.6 and 2.7, *The river of happy and sad and lonely feelings* and *The seed story*. They can use these pictures to explain to the child who it was that made the decisions about them coming into care and why. (See also Chapter 4: *Grief and loss* in the *Handbook* on pp 40–1 for ways to explain loss and also telling difficult stories in Chapter 7: *Helping children in transition* on pp 101–2.) Say that it is important to remember not to classify things as being "good" or "bad" because people just feel as they feel – the positive relationship we have with the child will allow the child to find the space to process their own loss.
- Sometimes a visit to the court or a re-enactment of the court procedure can help the child to work out who said what (especially birth parents). This then helps them to resolve why they came to live with this family.
- Suggest to participants they could also say something like:
  'Your parents loved you and made a beautiful child but were not able to keep you safe or care for you by feeding you regularly or taking you to school.'
  Or:
  'No one can take your memories and warm feelings away. Those feelings remain within us always; humans are lucky and can love many other people in our lives, the same way or in other ways, and this makes us feel lovable.'
  Or:
  'It was the grown-ups' responsibility to keep the children safe, but it's the child's responsibility to make good choices for themselves which are not worrying ones, for example, you choose red socks or green socks when you get dressed and wear the ones you like. It is a parent's responsibility to have plenty of dinner on the table and to share it equally. This shouldn't be *your* worry.'

The brick wall game

Tell participants that they can also use the brick wall game to help a child understand why they came into care – see No. 57 on the *Techniques CD*.

Remind participants that all carers and workers can help children express their feelings by putting them in touch with their senses, through offering them in their play different tastes, smells, and things to touch – maybe from their memory box. These can be added in during general daily life or at the specific time you are with them.

Say to participants that it's important that carers and children get to enjoy family times, such as preparing and eating meals together, or occasional days out that provide new experiences for the child. Having fun and gaining a skill is an essential part of feeling good about oneself and discovering both that you are unique and that you belong to a family or a group.

The silly senses game

Tell participants that they can use the silly senses game – see No. 50 on the *Techniques CD*. Other sensory games involve using music, things to touch like clay and paint, and food preparation. (It is helpful if you can go food shopping with young people and see if they can remember what their mum bought. If you can find recipes for meals they were familiar with, this can be a joint learning process and can create a change in the balance of power because the child will have to show you how to make them. This can also bring up many happy memories.)

For emotionally stuck children like Ryan, who need embodiment work (for example, re-experiencing his first years of life), you could use a baby basket and other early nurturing techniques. (See chapters on child development, attachment and play and the corresponding techniques on the CD.) Tell participants that using such techniques could be spread throughout the day's parenting.

Show Slide 14 to remind participants about the "four Fs" that describe the skills needed when working with children.

SLIDE 14
The Four Fs

What children need most of all is the following:
- Familiar...routines, regular warm patterns to the day, food, sleep, hugs
- Fun...a sense of humour, free play to explore and use imagination
- Firm...clear boundaries with empathy
- Friendly...to be heard with emotional warmth, have hugs, belong

(Corrigan and Floud, 1990)

Suggest to participants that physical activities like dance, sports, games, horse riding and drama can be helpful for children who are in a constant state of high arousal. As these activities rid the body of cortisol (the waste product of adrenalin), they can assist the child in regulating their feelings and in achieving, so that their self-esteem is enhanced.

Children may not always be able to concentrate for long so it is quite OK to break up a session with a burst of physical activity. This will also help them get in touch with their feelings and to begin to talk about their grief and losses.

Tell participants that more experienced workers can use sessions following the child's need (i.e. "free play" sessions). This often helps children discover their own story, which, if successful, can continue in each session as the child works in metaphor to process their own story while you reflect or play the part the child suggests. This gives the traumatised child some distance from the pain and they can more easily engage – see Chapters 8 and 9 on life history and therapeutic stories in the *Handbook*.

15 minutes   **7   DEMONSTRATION OF THE WATER GAME**

Explain to participants the water game (see No. 81 on the *Techniques CD*) and suggest how it might be used. Also, tell participants that it is a very powerful game and should be practised beforehand.

The purpose of the game is to demonstrate that feelings flow from one to another, and that parents support their child's emotional growth by keeping them full of love, as demonstrated by the topped-up water in their cup. By playing this game, the child can process their strong feelings and losses by filling or discarding the water in cups as needed. The child may be empowered to get angry and throw out the water belonging to, say, an abuser, which can be very healing and powerful and often frees the child's emotional growth and enables them to become unstuck.

Point out that there is no right or wrong way to play this game – the child will make it their own as they play with the water. The idea is simply to allow their play to reflect their feelings. Stress the need to use PACE and also to use humour as much as possible.

Point out that the game can be adapted by parents for adoptive children when they are in the bath – see details in the instructions for the water game, No. 81 on the *Techniques CD*.

After the game has finished, invite comments from the group.

15 minutes **8** ### EXERCISE: THE HAND-DRAWING GAME

The purpose of this game is to help the child think of, discuss and make a picture of their skills and achievements as well as their worries about the future. Participants can role play this so that they understand how to use it.

- Give participants some paper and ask them to find a partner.
- Then ask them to draw around each other's hands.
- Ask them to draw a bubble on top of each finger and then draw or write in it five things they like or have a talent for.
- Ask one partner to talk about things they would like to do in the future, while the other partner uses reflective listening and gives positive feedback.
- Tell participants that, when using this game with a child, they could finish by saying to the child, 'I wonder how you might get to do these things in real life.'

10 minutes **9** ### SELF-ESTEEM BUILDING TECHNIQUES

Tell participants that the following ideas can also be used to help the child gain self-esteem and to feel their own power and learn to regulate it.

- Create a DVD or photo storyboard of a child's life achievements and give them a means to store it, in the same way as you gave them a memory box.
- Give the child an address book or autograph book to record friends' names and numbers in, or a mobile phone (when they can manage this responsibly) to record numbers of friends and family that they are allowed to have contact with.
- Encourage the child from an early age to manage their pocket money as this teaches the child the value of money and gives them the power to control desire and wait for things, which is especially important for needy children. Tell participants that social workers are *in loco parentis* and it is part of their job to remind the parents/carers to help the children manage their pocket money.
- Use storytelling and help the child act out traditional stories they are familiar with from their particular cultural heritage, or imagine scenarios to help cope with bullying or name-calling. These, often metaphorical, stories can give the child an initial sense of anonymity, which enables them to reprocess their feelings and come to terms with fears before working on reality. It is also good to encourage the child to make up their own stories or poems, and to record these stories for them. You could also give them an opportunity to illustrate their stories with drawings or stickers, or you could take some photos of them dressed up as the

hero of the story (see Chapter 8, *Dramatic approaches to life history and surrounding issues* in the *Handbook*).

- You could maybe show participants the "nothing story" (see the book list in the *Handbook*), which is about a cat's lost identity that is regained; other children's books that use metaphor to explain how others have gained skills and coped with difficult situations are also listed. Say that, at the end of a session, it's good to help the child choose a short story that you read with them to sum up what you have been doing. It's amazing how the child's choice so often reflects the meaning the work has had for them and gives them closure.

Making a life orientation map

Explain to participants how to make a life orientation map by drawing one on flipchart paper – see No. 58 on the *Techniques CD* for instructions on this.

Allow some time for comments and questions from participants.

15 minutes | **10** | **EXERCISE: FAMILY TREE**

- Give participants paper and pens and ask them to draw out their own family tree going back two generations.
- Then ask them to get into pairs to share with their partner how easy or hard they found this and what else it made them feel as they did it.

One of their comments will probably be that they felt they didn't have enough information. Say that these things need research and time, which can be a problem when working with a child, but if you have filled in a flow chart during a careful assessment and at the same time asked the child questions about grandparents, taken any photos or copied them, you will have much to put into the life history book. The point here is that if direct work is begun from the moment the child comes into care, then life history facts and books are much easier to compile.

Draw participants' attention to the identity tree game in No. 77 on the *Techniques CD*.

Go on to talk about things that help children feel they belong:

- It is important first to help the child to know, or find out, who is in their birth family, and then who is in their foster or adoptive family.
- Tell them about their community/nationality (if relevant) and the world around them.
- If the child has moved from a town or from another country, look with them to find where that place is on a map and how that place connects to them now. Use Google Earth to find answers to these questions. (I have even found grandparents' farms!) The tourist office from the locality, usually found online, can also be useful in obtaining a history of the region and its culture.

10 minutes | **11** | **TALKING ABOUT DIFFERENCE AND HERITAGE**

Spend some time talking about heritage and difference – see Chapter 7: *Helping children in transition* in the *Handbook* under Talking about bodies and cultural difference (p. 87). You can add in here any relevant points that might not have come up in feedback in the case study on Ryan.

Looking at one's body

Tell participants about useful games that can help children with their feelings about their bodies (see the bodymap and silhouettes in Nos. 67 and 71 on the *Techniques CD*).

Tell participants that, if the child has a disability of any kind, whether visible or hidden, it is important to give them a chance to talk about the gains and losses in having a disability and to make it possible for them to fully participate in the activities arranged. As far as possible, they should make sure the child has access to up-to-date medical care, mobility and educational care, as this is often neglected.

Say that, however complex a child's needs are, it is important to help them recognise their competence – whether by simply teaching them to read, giving them a computer to communicate with, or providing a larger tray on their wheelchair so that a sand tray fits on it.

Explain to participants that part of self-esteem building is helping a child become aware of sexual health and about the facts of life (see pp 87–89 in Chapter 7: *Helping children in transition* in the *Handbook*). Many children in care do not have anyone to explain these facts properly to them, and provision at school is often not sufficient because they really need one-to-one help.

Tell participants about a book called *Mummy Laid an Egg* by Babette Cole (see the book list). This has a good explanation of the facts of life and is also very funny. However, clearly you must be aware of religious sensitivities and birth parents' wishes and feelings about when the facts of life should be shared.

5 minutes

12   DEMONSTRATION OF THE COUNTERS GAME

Before the lunch break, show how the counters game can be used to build up a parent's empathy for the child, as well as helping the child have empathy for themselves. Instructions for this can be found on the *Techniques CD* under *Neglect and trauma*, Game No. 23.

Explain to participants that "filial play" or "Theraplay" (for explanations see Chapter 5: *Play and communication* in the *Handbook*) can help a child catch up on lost nurture. It reduces stress and helps a child to improve regulation of his or her emotions and enhance identity and attachment building in new families. These techniques involve short, therapeutic 20-minute play times between a carer/parent and the child. These "play times" improve the experience of children who have had multiple losses and traumas, attachment problems and self-esteem issues. Users must be trained in certain skills and it takes 8 to 12 sessions to learn them and for the parent to be receiving good supervision. Some CAMHS services have a play therapist who is trained to teach filial play and who will supervise parents for a short time.

Remind participants to use techniques provided in *Managing Difficult Behaviour* or *Beyond Consequences and Control* (see the book list) to help them regulate children's emotions.

When to refer a child for specialist therapeutic help

Explain to participants that they may become aware that their direct work seems not to be having an effect as the child remains emotionally stuck and there is no change in their behaviour, even when the parents are also supporting the child (see Chapter 5: *Play and communication* under 'Training parents in therapeutic play' and 'Measuring progress using direct work').

If there is no sign of any change occurring, tell participants that they should make a referral to CAMHS, which usually has psychotherapists and play therapists. However, waiting times can be long and so it might be necessary to find a recommended private therapist on the websites of relevant professional associations, for example, the British Association of Play Therapists.

It is important to think carefully about what kind of therapy or activity is appropriate for a child or that this child is likely to engage with, i.e. think about what their talents are. For example, do they like to use play, music, art, practical manipulation, science-based tasks or sport? There are all kinds of different therapists working through drama, music with poetry, dance, art and "Theraplay". However, many therapists are person-centred and eclectic in their approach (i.e. are capable of combining ideas from many forms of therapy in their work).

1 hour	**13**	**LUNCH**

15 minutes	**14**	**INTRODUCTION TO LIFE HISTORY WORK**

Now tell participants that this afternoon you will be looking at how to work with children to record and process their life history.

Show participants Slide 15, referring to the Notes accompanying the slide.

SLIDE 15
Life history repair

- Where do I belong?
- Why do I need parents? Who is my dad?
- Why did I come into care?
- My past and present relationships

Introduce Slides 16, 17 and 18, pointing out the differences between birth parents and adoptive or other kinds of parents. The child needs to know that while substitute parents can give them many things, including love and care, no one but their birth parents can give them life itself and their genetic inheritance. This also helps children understand the consequences of what has happened to them and gives them a further chance to accept the loss of their birth parents as they unravel the difference through the direct work and play.

Thinking about birth parents

Say that participants may be faced with difficult questions from children about who their parents are, e.g. 'Who is my dad?' In such situations one needs to remind the child that their birth parents:

- gave them life itself;
- gave them their bodily appearance;
- gave them their many talents;
- taught them how to smile.

When we don't know who the child's father is, it is important to help the child to form a positive "construct" of a man. It can be useful to say something like:

I don't know who your dad was but he must have been a healthy man and his family may have been so too, because look how strong your legs are and how fast you can run. Your mum and dad were good at making a healthy child.

The important thing is to give the child the idea of a good father figure, so that they don't feel that they originate from someone who was intrinsically bad, or that men are to be feared. It can be useful to highlight the difference between the dad's strengths and his behaviour, if this is known. (You can find a list of ways to tell difficult stories in the *Handbook* in Chapter 7, *Helping children in transition*, on pp 101–2 and in Chapter 4: *Grief and loss* under "Yearning and pining". The egg drawing in No. 72 on the *Techniques* CD can also be helpful here.)

SLIDE 16
Where do I belong?

This is where we do in-depth life work with:
- Facts
- Feelings
- Fantasies
- Fears
  hopefully helping the child make some sense of his or her life and offering some help.

SLIDE 17
Why do I need parents?

SLIDE 18
Birth parents give you...

- Life itself
- Your sex
- Physical looks
- Intellectual potential
- Basic personality
- Talents
- Predisposition for diseases

Legal parents and parenting parents

Carry on with this work on distinguishing between birth and substitute parents by introducing participants to Slides 19 and 20, which describe the differences between legal parents and parenting parents.

SLIDE 19
Legal parent has responsibility for...

- Financial matters
- Safety and security
- Major decisions, e.g. where the child lives/goes to school
- Consent for operations
- Permission to travel
- Other legal consents

(Adapted from Fahlberg, 1994, p. 149)

SLIDE 20
Parenting parent gives you...

- Love
- Food
- Toys, clothes
- Help with schoolwork
- Hugs and kisses
- Discipline
- Care for you when you're sick
- Life skills and value

(From Fahlberg, 1994, p. 149)

Anxiety when starting life history work

Be aware that when introducing direct work on life stories, parents and workers are often anxious about where to start and sometimes claim that the child won't do the work. Suggest to participants that they "start small" by building up trust within the relationship and, as we have just done, starting with "identity" work and recording as we did this morning. Inevitably children will find life history work painful so those doing it with them must remember to use PACE, particularly using humour and avoiding setting up school-like sessions.

20 minutes   **15**   **EXERCISE: THE ORANGE GAME**

In order to engage participants after lunch, do the following exercise. This game offers a good way to introduce life history work to the older child.

Make the point that life history work can evoke strong feelings and so it is important that participants understand how it can feel – and this game can help. This game can be played with a child, as an introduction to thinking about what life history work really means. For this game you will need enough oranges and pieces of paper towel for each participant.

- Ask participants to find a partner.
- Give each participant an orange and ask them to spend two minutes imagining in their heads how the orange came to England: where it was born, how it left home, and how it came eventually to be in their hand.
- Say that they should then take it in turns to tell the story they have come up with to their partners. Allow about five minutes each for this.

- Then gather the group round in a big circle.
- Ask everyone to bite into their orange – and ask for feedback. They will probably say that they found it bitter. Point out that in the same way children find it tough to do life history work.
- Now ask them to peel the orange and share the pieces with each other. This is also hard to do. Participants may not want to pull it apart, especially as they have by now formed quite a friendly relationship with the orange and really would now prefer not to disturb it or give it pain. Doing this is a metaphor for probing the child. Sharing the child's history and pulling it apart is painful. But you should tell participants that pain is part of the cure in loss, and if you use PACE and listening skills, it gives the child a real opportunity to explore and understand their life history.
- Say that the work with the orange is a metaphor for what you are asking a child to do when starting life history work. Ask participants to think about how this makes them feel.

Feedback

You should allow about 10 minutes for feedback, as you will probably find that this game creates considerable discussion.

25 minutes   **16**   ## EXERCISE: THE FIRST MEMORY GAME

- Explain to participants that you will now show them another game that provides a way to start working with children doing life history work.
- Give participants coloured pens and paper.
- Say that participants should try to think of their first memory and draw it in a simple way for their partners, who will use reflective listening skills while they are drawing.
- Each partner shares their memories (using a toy if they want to) and is then invited by the listener to think about and perhaps draw another memory. Then they swap over.
- Explain to participants that they have 15 minutes to do this – about seven minutes each.

Below, I have provided my first memory to give you an idea of how this might work.

I remember getting my first set of cooking pans for my birthday when I was three years old and my mum cooked a fried egg in the miniature frying pan for my breakfast and she lifted me up to see it. I remember the brown crispy bits around the white of the egg and the black and white kitchen floor; it felt thrilling to be held safe and it was fun. The underlying message for those days in the 1950s was: "Girls stay in the kitchen". Thank goodness it's changed a lot since then, but it is still a happy memory. This highlights the fact that we have to be careful not to make value judgements about children's memories.

Feedback

Now spend five minutes collecting feedback from participants, as follows:

- How did they find the game?
- Were they surprised in any way by the outcome?
- Was it hard or easy?

Tell participants that, when doing this with children, it's a good idea to draw a memory of your own and then share it with the child, if they are finding it hard to get started. Or you could say something like, 'Some children remember the first time they got a present or went to the seaside.' This encourages the child to try to do the same and then more memories often tumble out.

Tell participants that a photo could be taken of the child drawing pictures and then be added to their life story book.

End by explaining that there are also other ways in which you can introduce life history work to children. For example, you might like to write their factual story as a metaphor using animal pictures as the characters. This can help the child ease their way into thinking about their story without too much pain. (For examples of therapeutic stories, see the "Nutmeg series" and others in the book list at the back of the *Handbook*.)

15 minutes　　**17　THINKING ABOUT HOW TO RECORD INFORMATION IN LIFE HISTORY WORK**

Now show Slides 21 and 22, which provide a summary of questions that the child is trying to gain answers to by doing the life history work. As you go through the slides, tell participants that they will find these on p. 91, Chapter 7 in the *Handbook*, and under "Life history headings" on the *Techniques CD*. Explain that the list on Slide 22 serves as questions for each page of the life history book, and by using these you and the child can find a way to explore the answers for you to then record. Other questions can, of course, be added.

SLIDE 21
Questions in life history

- Front page with child's name
- Who am I?
    - Identify facts
    - A copy of their birth certificate
    - A family tree
    - A moving map
    - A typical day in my life now
- What are my skills?
- What happened to me? i.e. where was I born?

SLIDE 22
Questions in life history

- What happened to me when I lived at home with Mum and Dad?
- What were my parents/siblings good at? What was their favourite food or music? What made them angry? What was the silliest thing they did?
- Why did I come into care?
- What has happened to me since I came into care?
- Who did I live with and what did I do or learn when with them?
- Who were my friends?
- What is a foster family compared with an adoptive family?
- If I am moving, what is the plan, who made it and why did they make it?
- Where am I going and why am I going there?

Pass around examples of any books you have brought along on life story work.

15 mins	18	**BREAK**

20 minutes   **19**   **DEMONSTRATION OF METHODS AND TECHNIQUES FOR LIFE STORY WORK**

Point out to participants where they can find ideas for life story work in the *Handbook* and *Techniques CD*.

Then go through the following to further explain important points to remember when doing life history work.

- Any writing in the child's life history book that you do on behalf of a child needs to be done in a style that is suitable for their age group. So, for example, the language used needs to be age appropriate. Equally, older children who have suffered trauma and deprivation will have had their education and vocabulary necessarily delayed, and you must be aware that they need to be able to read the book and feel confident about understanding it. Adding words from the child's own language (especially nurturing words) can be helpful. If the child has another first language, you should consider having the whole life history book translated. Alternatively, you could just translate the nurture words into the first language as they may be a trigger to positive emotional memory and healing.
- Remember that simple honesty is essential. Children are active participants in their lives at home – some things that happened were fun but others were not and pretending that everything was happy or easy is not helpful.
- It's important to remember that just as parents are responsible for their behaviour, so are older children over 10 years. They are not bystanders to their own lives and when they break basic rules they need to gradually own some responsibility and be aware that this has an effect on others. When doing repair work and recording information in books, acknowledge strong feelings and record ownership of behaviour on both sides in a gentle but honest way.
- When producing pages in the book, don't plasticise them but use plastic pockets to put them in instead. This is because the child may want to change the story as their perceptions of the world change. If there is a photo of an abuser included in the photos of special family members, put a cardboard door, which opens, over their picture so the child can choose whether or not they want to see that face when reading the book.
- All parents/carers will need to go over the information again and again with the child, as the child's perception of the world will change as they grow up in a safe placement. This process builds trust in their relationship and the child's sense of self-worth.
- By doing this life story work now, you could potentially reduce placement breakdown rates because the more emotionally available the child is and the better prepared, the easier the move and the process of reattachment.
- Photocopy all the books you make with a child or scan and store them on a CD and keep them on file, as good work and photos can often get lost or even deliberately destroyed.
- Record the book onto a CD for children who cannot read or are visually impaired, or have the book transcribed into Braille. Disabled children, very young children and learning-disabled children often find it easier to have the story in a cardboard book (see No. 62 on the *Techniques CD*) in which you have stuck different textures to express feelings: like sandpaper

to express when times were rough, or soft fur to express a cosy feeling. Put the story on a CD or DVD and add music.

Tell participants that sometimes it's hard for the child to write or think about the past and you can illustrate this with the following case study.

> 'I don't like to think about that house,' said Hannah after she and her worker had done a lot of painful life history work and were thinking about recording it. 'I don't want to draw it.'
>
> The worker replied: 'What about making a collage of a mess or a scribble drawing of a mess so when you are looking at it you will know what it's about and how you feel, but no one else has to know the details. We could put the words "a painful mess" or just "a mess" under it. That way you can now say "no" to all that went on there.'
>
> Hannah smiled and she enthusiastically made a huge mess on the page representing pain and worry. She told her worker about it again while she drew it, putting each bit of "coloured rubbish" in a messy pile that represented her feelings to her.
>
> In this way Hannah gained mastery of what had happened and realised that she was a hero of her own story and had survived.

- You can also make a DVD of a child achieving something like skipping or jumping in a puddle so they have a concrete story that they really understand is theirs. Real video material with pictures inserted can help a child understand that they are the hero of that story. This is especially good for reinforcing self-esteem.
- Think about who will be doing or supervising the different parts of this work. If you have no specialist supervisor available, join up for pair supervision with another parent or colleague whom you respect, especially someone you value for his or her common sense. It really helps to have someone else to think with you.

Demonstrate some of the following:

- Show participants the "road map on canvas" – see No. 61 on the *Techniques CD*. Demonstrate this on paper and show a photo of a canvas one. (Say that the advantage of canvas maps is that they can be used over and over again for all sorts of play and processing of life history – and for when a child has moved house (by adding new and old houses to it and other toy cars or figures)).
- Tell participants that, when the child's siblings are not living with them, the places those siblings live in need also to be recorded on the map so the child gets a sense of place or country. These should be shown connected by road, air or sea.
- Another idea when the child is reluctant to start is for the worker to begin by drawing some scenery, like roads, hills and houses. They could invite the children to add to the picture, either by drawing or adding toys on top of the worker's scenery and then being invited to tell a story connected to them. Photograph the picture and add it to the life story book with the child's comments.
- Tell participants to make a time-line with the child (see No. 73 on the *Techniques CD*), using graph paper to show how long they stayed in each place, continuing into adoption. Their adoptive home soon becomes the home in which they have spent the most time and this is very reassuring for those who are frightened of abandonment.

- To answer the question How long am I staying?, do the toilet-roll game (No. 1 on the *Techniques CD*). Take the child on visits to places like their old school or places where they lived, or even where they were born. Give the child a disposable camera to record this trip. You will find that they love going into the local shop or chatting, for example, to their old dinner ladies because these people remember them and this often boosts their self-esteem and also reminds them why they are living in a substitute family. If you take a sibling group, you need one adult per two children, not only for safety but also in order to be available to listen to their memories and to record them. Trips help to remind children of the funny things that happened as well as the sad ones. It's important to remember that children have had happy times too, even if they have come into care. However, only do trips to old home areas if it is safe to do so (to avoid contact with previous abusers).
- Show participants books like *Life Story Work*, *My Life and Me*, *Chester and Daisy Move On*, *Life Story Books for Adopted Children* and *Telling the Truth to your Adopted or Fostered Child*.
- Help children to decorate the pages of their life story book with stickers, pictures or poems, or make up a music compilation that the child can put on when they are reading the story. This might be their special music they listen to at home, but it needs to be their choice.
- It can be good to help teenagers make a DVD film of their story, as they will enjoy doing this. If you work with teenagers you could also run a group for working on life stories because they can help each other this way, and it also makes them aware that others have gone through similar experiences.
- Encourage children to play out some of their experiences via sand tray stories, drama stories with puppets or dressing up as the characters in it.

20 minutes **20** ## EXERCISE: FEARS ABOUT DOING DIRECT WORK

- Ask participants to get into groups and discuss for 5 minutes what fears or problems they might have with actually helping children with these ideas and questions.
- Ask them to write these down on flipchart paper.
- Then discuss these in the larger group for 10 minutes.
- Go through participants' fears and anxieties, reflecting these back using listening skills to model how one would do this with children.
- Participants' worries are often about time, or the difficulties of listening to a child's pain and managing their behaviour. Tell them that listening to a child is the secret to getting children to move on, as the fact of being heard helps them gain the courage to do this work.

Hold a discussion about the practical aspects of this work, for example:

- getting hold of the right equipment;
- doing direct work under time constraints.

Suggest to participants that they try just one client at a time. Get permission from their manager and try with the under-eight-year olds to start with. In this case the worker will obviously have to make the books for the children or use a template format (as in *My Life and Me*) but young children love to add stickers and to go on trips, etc. and they will teach you how to pace the work and give you confidence to do it with an older group (who can be more challenging to handle and more fixed in their view of what happened). Using the statutory visits over time, work with the child for 30 minutes or so before offering the parent support.

Suggest they practise techniques with a co-worker in order to help them process their fears.

Finally, suggest that they read Part 2: After the court case on p. 91 in the *Handbook* and Preparing for a move, to give them increased confidence to be able to deal with the child's questions.

10 minutes **21** **FINAL POINTS**

10 minutes   **21**   **FINAL POINTS**

Say to participants that children's lives have often been so chaotic that it can be hard to make sense of what happened without the worker giving the child real practical and emotional support. Sometimes the child may dictate to you what they want to say, or add a sticker or pictures, or possibly cross something out angrily. This is all fine because the book is a joint effort – it doesn't have to look perfect and it needs to be owned by the child.

Always try to be honest if a child asks difficult questions, and if you don't know the facts, then don't make them up. Just put into the book the child's memory of the moment without making it into something good or bad. When explaining again to a child about why they have come into care, you might need to say simply that 'after thinking about it a lot, a judge said you should come into care and have new parents'. Other relatives can be helpful in explaining to children what really happened to them. (See *Dennis Duckling* and *Dennis and the Big Decisions*, both picture books that help explain why Dennis duckling came into care and the decision-making process about where Dennis was to live (see book list at the back of the *Handbook*).)

When doing life history work it is better to help the child to come to terms with what they remember, whilst helping them find a way of accepting what you know. Helping the child to find a compromise in this way can build up their resilience. The child accepts the past but can move on, strong in the knowledge that the worst has happened and they now have the support of the new parents you have found for them and with whom, one hopes, they will have the confidence to share their story.

The child's story will continue to evolve and change over their life and so it's important to leave space in the book for the next few years. It can also be useful to give the child their own photo album with carefully chosen photos – one that doesn't have the story written in it so they can show the photos to their friends without being embarrassed.

Tell participants that the following themes often come up in children's play:

- Good versus evil
- Being kidnapped/rescued
- Feeling overwhelmed/experiencing loss/near-death experiences
- Place of safety/survival and recovery
- Deserving/undeserving
- Fear of inadequacy (after telling off)
- Aggression/power/oppression
- Trickery/telling the truth
- Rehearsal for living, re-nurturing and other forms of practising growing up.

Tell participants to look in the *Handbook* at Chapter 6 on play and Chapters 8 and 9 on stories and drama to help find ways to help a child process these themes and find resolution.

Finally, explain that, when playing with children, you can help them by thinking of different ways to solve a problem or an alternative resolution to a story: 'I was wondering if you could think of another way to end this story?' Eventually, by thinking together with the child (but not by instructing them), you can give the child the ability to problem-solve and to avoid always viewing their past life as a tragedy. This way they can be helped to find resolution as they change endings from disaster to hope. However, it's important always to remember that this can only happen if the child has been allowed to go through the grieving process first and that they can often only come to terms with this when in a permanent placement. Suggest to participants that they look at Nos. 32, 33, 51 and 52 on the *Techniques CD* for ways to start this kind of storytelling.

5 minutes   **22   CLOSING THE SESSION**

End the session by asking one or two people in the group to say one thing they might have learned or gained from the session and express the hope that they are looking forward to the next session, when you will be looking at moving children into new placements.

SESSION 4
Moving and re-attachment

OVERVIEW

	Section	Timing
1	Welcome and goals for Session 4	**10 minutes**
2	Exercise: *Moving*	**30 minutes**
3	Presentation on moving children	**5 minutes**
4	Exercise: *Moving children into new families*	**30 minutes**
5	Feedback on the case study exercise about Jade	**15 minutes**
6	Break	**15 minutes**
7	Feedback on the case study exercises about Rio & Pio and Joshua	**75 minutes**
8	The four seasons exercise and the soft toy story	**30 minutes**
9	Lunch	**1 hour**
10	Candle ceremony demonstration	**25 minutes**
11	Group discussion: Supporting families during moves	**25 minutes**
12	Exercise: *Contact*	**15 minutes**
13	Break	**15 minutes**
14	Exercise on study child	**40 minutes**
15	Final exercise	**20 minutes**
16	Bring course to a close	**10 minutes**

PREPARATION

You will need to read Part 3 of Chapter 7: _Helping children in transition_ in the _Handbook._

PARTICULAR RESOURCES NEEDED FOR THIS SESSION

- The PowerPoint presentation for Session 3.
- A paper or canvas moving map you have prepared (see No. 61 on the _Techniques CD_).
- Some card books as described in No. 62 on the _Techniques CD_ or show photos of them.
- Copies of the following books: _Chester and Daisy Move On; Dennis Duckling_ and an example from the Nutmeg series – see the book list in the _Handbook;_ also books on the BAAF website on talking to children about adoption
- Some paints and paintbrushes, or felt-tip pens and paper
- The soft toy participants have brought to previous sessions
- Equipment for a candle ceremony – see No. 26 on the _Techniques CD_
- Enough copies for each participant of the "toy bag" drawing given out in Session 1
- Optional: some children's sweets or some cake to share as they do the toy bag exercise
- Evaluation sheets about the course to give out at the end of the day

HANDOUTS

- 4.1 _Session 4 Overview_
- 4.2 _Case studies on Jade, Rio & Pio and Joshua_
- 4.3 _The soft toy story_
- 4.4 _Dialogue for a candle ceremony_
- 4.5 _Additional listening skills_
- 4.6 Evaluation sheets
- A printout of the PowerPoint presentation

10 minutes

1   WELCOME AND GOALS FOR SESSION 4

Put up Slide 1.

SLIDE 1
Moving and re-attachment

Welcome everyone back, and remind the group of the ground rules. Briefly take participants through what they learnt in the previous session on identity and life history work and ask if there were any thoughts as a result. Discuss these as time allows.

Show Slide 2 and go through the goals for the day with the participants.

SLIDE 2
Goals for the day

- To think about how moves and changes affect us
- To learn how to move children without trauma
- To think about how we start this work
- To think about how to help children attach to new families after separation

30 minutes **2** **EXERCISE: MOVING**

Put up Slide 3 and explain that the purpose of this exercise is to remind participants that moves can be painful, and can trigger all kinds of emotions. However, we can gain skills as a result of moves and changes and can become resilient. Nonetheless, too many moves can knock us down completely. This means that *how* we prepare or move children is crucial to how they recover from this change, and ultimately how safe they feel with adults.

Ask participants to read the instructions on the slide.

Then hand out a sheet of paper to each participant and ask him or her to individually answer the questions on the slide. Ask them to take an example from their own childhood, like a school or house move. If participants look uncertain when asked to do this, you can give them an example from your own childhood or a case study to get them thinking.

Tell them that when you share feedback on this you will only ask them what *feeling* they had when they made this move and what *skill* (i.e. became confident and thus independent) was positively or adversely affected. (Remind them only to share what they feel comfortable sharing.)

Give them 5–10 minutes in which to do this.

SLIDE 3
A move in your life

Exercise: Think of a move or change in your life
- Where were you?
- Who were the people who helped or hindered you?
- Any skills that were adversely or positively affected?
- How did you feel?

In the meantime, draw two columns on the flipchart, one headed "feelings" and one headed "skills".

When the group has finished, take feedback. Ask them to share their feelings, whether negative or positive, and write these up.

Then ask for the skills they think they gained or lost as a result of the move. Write these up on the flipchart as you work round the group.

At the end, sum up by saying that moves can change things, and we can be helped or hindered by friends and family. If the move is not sudden and the child is well prepared for it, they can gain small amounts of resilience and confidence to manage the change and this builds their self-esteem.

5 minutes **3** **PRESENTATION ON MOVING CHILDREN**

Explain to participants that, however settled a child has been in foster care, moving causes them to regress to previously learnt traumatic or reactive behaviours. They are worried that they are going to move back into the anxiety and pain of the past. Moving sets off grief reactions. For example, triggers such as the smell of autumn can remind them of a previous move. Their behaviour can often appear inexplicable: the child can withdraw, have a nervous tummy, wet him or herself or be angry. They may also not be able to stop chatting, or may become hyperactive.

Introduce and discuss Slide 4, using the Notes that accompany the slide.

SLIDE 4
Moving – Part 1

● Who gives permission?
● Understanding the child's idea of time
● Devising a clear plan

Now show Slide 5, using the Notes provided.

SLIDE 5
Moving – Part 2

● Who will be supervising the different parts of this work?
● What is the timescale?
● Who will continue the work, going over it again and again when the child is in a safe placement?
● How do we know when our direct work is not helping? When should we refer to a specialist?

30 minutes **4** ## EXERCISE: MOVING CHILDREN INTO NEW FAMILIES

Tell participants that they will now spend 30 minutes on an exercise that involves looking at case studies of children, and they can choose a case study that relates to the age group they are particularly interested in working with/more commonly need to work with.

Tell them that these cases are about children of different ages:

● Jade is aged 18 months. *This case study is for a group interested in looking at a child aged 0–2 years.*
● Rio is six years old and Pio is four. *This case study is for a group interested in looking at children aged 2–8 years.*
● Joshua is 11. *This case study is for a group interested in looking at older children.*

Participants need to consider and answer the questions under each case study.

Say that once they have chosen which age group they would like to think about, they should get into three groups to do the exercise. Give out the three case studies in Handout 4.2.

Tell participants that once the exercise has been completed, you will go through each case study, taking feedback, and you will add ideas as you go along. At the beginning of each case study feedback, you will need to ask one participant to read the case out loud for everyone to hear, as participants will only have seen the case study for the group they are working in.

5   FEEDBACK ON CASE STUDY EXERCISE ABOUT JADE

Before the break it's important that you take feedback on the case study about Jade as she is only 18 months old and each age group in the case studies follows on from this one and so you won't need to repeat demonstrations of techniques.

Ask the group that looked at the case study about Jade to read the case study out loud and then to say what their answers were. Then, if they have not covered the issues below, point these out, together with anything else you consider relevant from your own practice or from 'Moving to a permanent family' (p. 98) in Chapter 7: *Helping children in transition* of the *Handbook*.

Possible answers to the questions about Jade are as follows:

1. How would you prepare Jade for a move?

The social worker can explain to Jade that she is 'changing mummies and daddies' by using two houses with beds and blankets saying, 'This is foster mum's (use her name) house and this is new mummy and daddy's (use name) house'. Then drive a car containing a doll to show the child having a sleepover and coming back. Show her a picture of the new parents. In this way you can familiarise the child with the impending move, and although the child won't quite understand it at that age, it is not so scary when it actually happens, as they have understood at an unconscious level that this is somehow safe.

The new parents need to spend every day with Jade in the foster carers' house getting used to routines and doing the caring for Jade by using attachment games and learning skills from the foster carers, until Jade feels easily comforted by them without anxiety. Show the participants the book *The Teazles' Baby Bunny*, which is useful in explaining adoption for children aged up to about four. See also the book list at the back of the *Handbook* and on www.baaf.org.uk/bookshop.

2. What could the foster carer do to help this whole process?

When preparing Jade or a baby for a move, foster carers can repeat the social worker's story by acting it out with two little toy people and a toddler and with two sets of beds in two houses. Rehearsal is the key to reducing pain. It can also help to read books to children about moving, even though the child does not always understand the words.

The foster carers could also wash the new bed linen belonging to the adopters/kinship carers in their own soap powder and arrange for the child to sleep in it one night before he or she goes to the adopters for good, so the bed smells the same as the one in the new home. Bottle teats and dummies should be handed over too, as the child is used to those. Transitional objects like blankets, puppets or teddy bears should also be used to accompany the child on any journey to, for example, the park. Spraying the perfume the foster carer uses onto the bear also helps to make the child feel secure. The social worker could suggest to the foster carer that they give a cotton cloth with her perfume on it to put over the shoulder of the adoptive parent when nursing babies.

3. How would the adopters become familiar with the child's routine and how long would introductions take?

The typical moving time allowed for a baby is one week of intensive introductions. It is most important to help adopters mirror the patterns of the foster carer's body language, routines and ways of soothing and caring for the infant, at the beginning of the placement and in their own home. Changes can be made to routines later on when child attachment is evident – for example, when the baby smiles, babbles with the mother and is easily regulated and comforted by the new parents, as we saw in Session 1 in the film on attachment (if shown).

4. What contact goodbye arrangements would you make with the carer?

The social worker can set up contact arrangements after placement between the foster carer and the adoptive parents. It is usual to see the child at least once after placement. On the first day of a new placement, it is helpful for the adoptive parent to make a phone call to the carer to say how the child is settling. If need be, contact can take place via phone until the situation is routine and any minor problems are sorted out. Within six weeks of the placement, it is helpful for all concerned if the foster carer can come on a short visit to the new home to see that the child is settled and safe. If this visit goes well, the carer can let go more easily and take on new children, and the adopters get validated in their parenting skills, which enhances confidence and their attachment to the child. The child also gets the message that the foster carer "approves" and has given permission for the child to move on.

| 15 minutes | 6 | **BREAK** |

| 75 minutes | 7 | **FEEDBACK ON THE CASE STUDY EXERCISES ABOUT RIO & PIO AND JOSHUA** |

Ask the group that looked at the case study of Rio and Pio first to read the case study aloud to the rest of the group and then feedback their answers.

Then do the same with the group that looked at Joshua's case study.

If necessary, supplement the answers that participants give with the information given below.

Questions about Rio and Pio

How would you prepare the children for adoption before knowing there was a family? What could the social workers and foster carers do in practice to prepare them when a family was identified?

(See also Part 3 (p. 98) in Chapter 7: *Helping children in transition* in the *Handbook*.)

Since the social worker already knows that these children are to be placed for adoption, preparation for the move and introducing the idea of adoption should be within the context of doing their life history with them in the statutory visits, as discussed in Session 3.

Once the social worker knows that there is a family in the frame, usually about four weeks before the matching panel, then in conjunction with the carer it is a good idea to start playing with each child about what it might be like to have a new mummy and daddy. Use a life orientation map or the river or seed story drawings to introduce them to the idea that they might move in future. Using the canvas map technique or a cardboard roadmap with different houses on it, imagine aloud with each child how it would be to go on visits to a new house. What might be in it? Are there toys or pets? What would be their worries about changing families? As mentioned earlier, rehearsal is the key to managing change and really reduces the stress for the child. For children of this age, having done the life history part of the work, four weekly sessions is about enough time to get them used to the facts and to explore some of their fears about a move.

Once the matching panel has agreed that this is a good match, the social worker is able to start to tell the child that they have found a "forever family". They can tell the child via a little picture book, which the adopters are encouraged to have prepared. (See *Me and My Family*, published by BAAF in 2011 – a colourful book which the child and adopters can use to get to know each other better.) The social worker will be able to show the children pictures of the person/people who will come and visit the following day, when they will be introduced.

Make a point of accepting any odd behaviour the children show. Help them to express their feelings, and avoid labelling these as good or bad. Children need to be able to say, 'I don't want to go' without you saying, 'It will be fine.' Allow them their strong feelings and talk about the fears and strangeness of it all. 'Will I be safe?' is often an unspoken fear. Go through worries with them about things like bedtime routines, lights on at night, trying out the toilet (can they go to it at night?), what and how much they will be able to eat, and so on. Show participants books like *Chester and Daisy Move On* or the Nutmeg stories (see the book list in the *Handbook*).

How long would the introduction to new parents take?

In general, the new parents visit the children at the carers' home and gradually take over the care, and by about the tenth day a sleepover in the new house is arranged. As the children are introduced to the new home, they take more and more of their belongings to put in their bedroom so that it begins to feel more like home.

Then there is a mid-introduction meeting with all concerned, at which all parties share how the child is coping. The new parents are then asked if they feel they can commit to the children. If this is agreed, the introductions continue and the placement goes ahead.

It is essential and good practice that the workers have all talked to their clients about this commitment prior to the mid-term meeting. Children of this age are usually placed within about a week of this mid-term meeting, so in all it takes two-and-a-half to three weeks to place children of this age for adoption. Adopters are usually asked to collect children on the final day from the foster carers, so the children don't feel they have been abandoned again but have been chosen.

How could the adopters prepare themselves and what could they do to ease this transition for the children? Can the social worker help in any way?

If adopters have never played with young children for any length of time, then working in a nursery class or babysitting or offering to help at a local school really does familiarise them with the pressure and what they can expect. Going on a parenting course to help with boundary setting can also be very helpful. It should not be underestimated how hard it is to take on traumatised children, as it takes at least two years for them to properly settle and feel safe. The adopters should also establish good networks of support that are dependable for respite and support.

In some situations, social workers should be able to offer real financial and practical help, for example, to ease this transition when a sibling group is taken on or a child has very particular needs.

How would you prepare an ending in the placement? What contact visits would you arrange between the foster carers and the new parents and children?

Arrange a contact visit within six weeks with carers and the new family, in a neutral place like a cafe or park, so that the foster carer could, for example, bring some of her other children and they can all play together. Rio and Pio will then see that the foster carer still has her job to do and they have attentive parents of their own supporting their play. This helps to accept and manage the separation. Keep contact if wished, with occasional phone calls and gradually reduce them, unless both sides want a yearly meet-up, as in the case of carers who feel like the children's real aunt and uncle now.

(See Chapter 7: *Helping children in transition* in the *Handbook* for suggestions on ways to end placements.)

Questions about Joshua

What could the social worker and foster carer do to prepare Joshua for a move and the loss of his siblings?

When doing his life history during the identity part of the work, Joshua should be helped to feel that he has needs and then to discover that he is deserving of these needs being met. In this part of the work, he could be helped to understand the separate and different needs of his siblings. It can be difficult to engage Joshua's age group (11) in direct work, but if the metaphors are active or drama is used, it is easier for them to see what their situation is. Many young people in his situation settle in their placement only when they can see that their siblings are settled. It is essential that the new parents of the other children accept that he has had a parental role, and if they refer to his previous role with respect, it will make contact easier. Say to participants that the use of the candle ceremony as part of this work can be an excellent means of helping with loss and anger and can be done over and over again, as will be demonstrated this afternoon.

How would you organise introductions?

In a similar way to what was suggested for Rio and Pio.

How long would they take?

In the older group these introductions can be spread over weekends for about a six-week period but in reality, as soon as the young person has decided that he could make a go of it in this new family and he has accepted the inevitable, they usually vote with their feet and end up just staying after one weekend because they hate goodbyes.

What contact arrangements would you make for Joshua with his siblings?

Sibling contact should be gradually reduced to a practical amount: usually what works in practice is once in the half-term and in each holiday – reducing from six to three times a year especially as Joshua gets older. But it very much depends on what his new parents think is in Joshua's best interests and how Joshua gets on with his siblings and their new carers. As they all grow and change, so the nature of contact will change.

General points about making moves easier

Tell participants that the following points are useful to tell foster carers.

- Give the child a calendar on which is marked the times of the visits to the new parents and when the new parents are going to telephone on the other days.
- Give the young child a sticker box so they can add one each day. In this way a child with poor understanding of time can keep checking on what's happening and this reduces their anxiety.
- Join in the child's happiness when looking over their life history book, videos of achievements or certificates, or future plans. Rehearsal and preparation for a move is really important: using drama with puppets and dolls can be really useful to reduce a child's fear and anxiety. For withdrawn children, go back to using sensory play, i.e. warm play dough, clay, cooking and sand play. Show them via play that there will be food, a cosy bed, a night-light and a clean toilet, etc.
- Children often feel 'I had to move because I was naughty'; they feel ashamed, guilty, have poor self-esteem, and often become angry. Tell carers always to remember that the child is not bad, but full of fear, and so not to isolate them when they or the carer are angry. Tell carers to use another space near them in their house for a "time out", like a big cosy armchair.
- The social worker and family finder, along with the matching panel, are responsible for finding the right family and match. The child needs to know this is not up to them. Children with an avoidant-style attachment think they need to control the world to make it safe so often feel responsible for everything, including whether this placement is right for their siblings.
- The child's foster carer/residential worker must be allowed to express feelings about whether this family is the right match for the child. They may also need support with their own grief at losing the child.
- It is good practice to share the life history aloud with new parents in front of the child before a move so the child understands that the parents know and accept his or her history.
- Both sides – the child and the new family – must be allowed to express, share and show that they feel the family is right. If one or other doesn't feel it is right, then they should be given time and space to express these fears to an experienced worker who understands whether this is a relevant fear from the past (of the child) or a fear to do with the carer's past and therefore not actually to do with the child.
- The adopters must also say, and show the child, in the process of introductions, that they welcome and want this child to be part of their family before actually having the child to stay permanently. They can do this by saying something like: 'We enjoyed today and we are really looking forward to you being part of our family.'

Remind participants of the loving and caring water activity in Session 3 (see No. 81 on the *Techniques CD*) as this helps process moves and feelings about moves. Tell them you will also show them the candle ceremony later in the day, which is helpful when trying to practise the idea of letting go as it is a goodbye ceremony.

| 30 minutes | 8 | **THE FOUR SEASONS EXERCISE AND THE SOFT TOY STORY** |

You should now take participants either through the four seasons exercise or make up a story using soft toys if you have time.

● Instructions for the four seasons exercise can be found in No. 74 on the *Techniques CD*. The purpose of this exercise is to show the child that, even though they have been through a very difficult year, they can gain things from it and make a new start.

● If you decide instead to make up a story with the soft toys participants have brought, then see Handout 4.3, which gives instructions on this. The purpose of this activity is to give participants practice in interacting with children by using metaphor. This will make it easier for them to imagine with the child what it might be like to find resolution to their story.

Allow 25 minutes for whichever of these you choose to do.

● Then spend five minutes asking participants for feedback on what they thought of the technique.

| 1 hour | 9 | **LUNCH** |

| 25 minutes | 10 | **CANDLE CEREMONY DEMONSTRATION** |

Show participants Slide 6 as background to the next two exercises, starting with the candle ceremony.

Remind participants that they first saw this slide in Session 2. Say that while you demonstrate the candle ceremony, which helps children process loss, participants should think about which stage of the loss process the child in the demonstration is going through.

SLIDE 6
The six-stage model of bereavement and the effects of secondary trauma

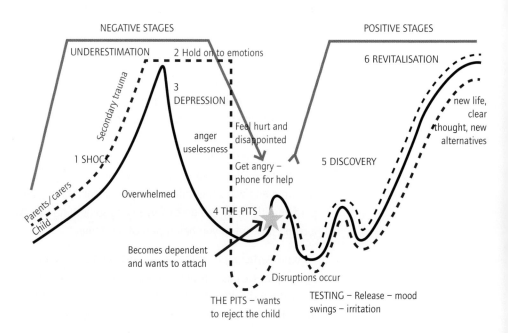

The candle ceremony

For this, use Handout 4.4, *Dialogue for a candle ceremony*. The whole exercise takes about 20 minutes to carry out. You will find the method to be used for this, including the safety rules, in No. 26 on the *Techniques CD*.

Find a participant to take the role of the child in this exercise, one who hasn't yet lost a grandmother. This dialogue is about losing a grandmother, who dies when the child is only three-and-a-half, and who therefore can't quite verbalise her loss.

Once you have finished the exercise, discuss with the group when they might use this technique and what they think about it.

Tell participants that it can be used in many ways:

- helping with a loss after a death;
- when a child is coming into care;
- for ending a final session with a child; or
- simply as a means by which powerful feelings can be expressed.

25 minutes

11 GROUP DISCUSSION: SUPPORTING FAMILIES DURING MOVES

Explain to participants that, when supporting the care plan, the aims of permanent placement are to:

- help the child to form a new secure attachment;
- help the child to have a secure base from which they can recover from loss;
- provide a place where the child can feel they belong so they can develop good self-esteem and a sense of identity.

As a result the child will be able to problem-solve for themselves, gain resilience and develop their talents.

Now lead a large-group discussion with participants on how we can help a family form new attachments, and how we can support families during moves – see the list of games on the *Techniques CD* under *Child development and attachment*.

As you do this, go through Slide 6 to remind participants of the process the child and family are going through whilst moving. List the ideas on the flipchart as you go along.

If necessary, supplement participants' ideas with the following:

- Listen to the child's grief and the carer's parallel worries/grief. (Mention here that adoptive parents often grieve for their lost unborn child, or a fantasy child, and that having an adopted child can bring an old loss to the fore.)
- Use advice and ideas in the *Handbook* in Chapter 3: *Neglect and trauma* and Chapter 4: *Grief and loss* and on the *Techniques CD* to help in the first weeks and after the child is over the first shock.
- New parents can practise getting physically close to the child with games like Twister, reading stories, sharing play activities like blowing bubbles, playing ball or balloons, the trust game (see *Child development and attachment* on the *Techniques CD*) and swimming. Cook and share food, give hot chocolate before bed, read stories and have rest and cosy times.
- For some children who have an ambivalent or avoidant attachment style, being close can actually feel very new and scary. Take time before you touch them and use a doll or teddy to

demonstrate how you would like to behave towards them rather than insisting on hugs too early. (Demonstrate this to participants by picking a teddy up and wrapping him in a blanket, giving him a hug whilst talking to him.)

- For really scared children, putting up a little tent in the sitting room (e.g. a pop-up one from Ikea) can provide a safe place if the child needs a cosy quiet time (rather like being back in the womb). Close experiences, like massaging hands and feet, can also be helpful. For older children, brush their hair or change hairstyles, paint their faces with face paint or try out painting fingernails.
- Watching TV or a favourite DVD/film, or playing computer games, can give a child emotional rest from the pain of a move. Be close to them and reduce the time spent doing this very gradually.
- Doing the water game is helpful in reducing a child's anxiety.
- Use Handout 4.5, *Additional listening skills*. (These are healing and feeling play ideas and are listed on the *Techniques CD*.) Go through these with participants.
- Continue your repair life history work, enabling the new parents to become involved with any work you do so they can be openly accepting of the past and so that together the child and the whole family begin their own history – refer participants to the ideas in Chapters 7–9 of the *Handbook*.
- Spend time with both sets of parents, listening to their anxieties, helping them discover their own solutions to supporting their new children.
- Providing practical financial help from the post-adoption support service budget can be useful.
- If parents are experiencing emotional difficulties with their own issues about not having birth children, coupled with the reality of taking on traumatised children, suggest they seek professional help as this can only help themselves as well as the child.

If time, demonstrate or play with the group an attachment game found in the list on the *Techniques CD* under *Child development and attachment*.

15 minutes | **12** | **EXERCISE: CONTACT**

Divide participants into equal groups.

Ask participants to think about how they would plan and decide on the type of contact that would be appropriate for:

- each past family member;
- the child in an adoptive home; or
- kinship carers.

Write up the following questions on the flipchart for participants to try to answer.

What is the purpose of the contact?

- Possible answers include:
  - To reassure the child that birth parents/relatives still care about him/her.
  - To enable a child to grieve his/her loss and so move on.
  - To provide a chance for the child to gain greater knowledge and understanding about who they are and where they came from.
  - To help a child develop an attachment to his/her new parents.
  - To establish a sense of continuity and strengthen the sense of self.

What difficulties might arise during and after contact?

- Possible answers include:
    - The child could become distressed or confused.
    - The child could feel disappointed or let down.
    - Birth parents may give ambivalent messages such as, 'I am going back to court to get you back' or 'I love you, you are still my child', rather than saying something like, 'I still love you but because I couldn't care for you, I am happy for you to have a family to love and care for you.' If birth parents persist in reinforcing negative messages, then contact is not in the child's best interest and will need to be reviewed.
    - Some birth parents have few boundaries and if there is sexual abuse in the background, the contact must be closely supervised. If face-to-face contact *is* recommended, you have to carefully consider whether the positives outweigh the negatives in situations when children might come into contact with a relative who might have hurt or abused one or more of the siblings.

How often and where might visits take place?

- Possible answers are that:
    - The court gives an order about the number of contact visits the child should have but if it's left to the local authority's discretion, then three times a year is about the maximum a child can manage if they are to feel their home is with their adoptive parents. Once a year may be enough because children often regress after contact and it needs time and patience to help them through it.
    - For siblings, three to four times a year can help the child feel a continuity with the past as well as secure in the present.
    - Appropriate venues for contact meetings can be a café, park or other neutral settings that offer a containing safe place with really fun things to do, not an office setting. Supervised contact can take place in a family centre, for example.

What is letterbox contact and who is supposed to write the letter? Give some pointers to what should be in it.

- Possible answers include:
    - Letterbox contact is an exchange of information – letters, cards, photographs – between the adoptive family and birth family, about the child. Gifts from the birth parents are not encouraged.
    - It can be a two-way exchange but birth parents may find it difficult to comply, so generally it is the adoptive parents who will send a letter and a photograph of the child once a year.
    - The letter could contain information about how the child is settling in, significant milestones, how the child is getting on at school, etc.
    - In cases of large sibling groups, it could be useful to put together and circulate a newsletter (each parent contributing a photo and a little bit about the child) for siblings to read.

Sum up with the following suggestions if participants have not made them.

- Don't forget that babies and very young children may also need face-to-face contact as they will also miss their family but won't be able to say so prior to adoption.
- Think about who is supervising the contact. This job is usually allocated to the post-adoption team or specialist worker. Is this possible in your area?

- Don't make contact sessions too long – 1.5 hours is about as much as most children can manage without getting upset (which then causes old behaviours and fears to reappear).
- If these contacts are with birth parents, it is often helpful if there is a support person to talk to them before and after the contact, especially when establishing this kind of contact. Birth parents often need to be reminded that this contact is intended to be in the children's best interests and not their own.
- Contact arrangements need regular review as children's views and their understanding of the world changes over the years.
- Children's behaviour may completely change as a result of contact. Reasons to stop contact altogether include the passing of inappropriate messages to the child, and unhelpful behaviour being modelled, such as being drunk or consistently failing to turn up over a long period.
- Letterbox contact can work very well if it is too stressful for all concerned to have contact face-to-face, for whatever reason.

| *15 minutes* | **13** | **BREAK** |

| *40 minutes* | **14** | **EXERCISE ON STUDY CHILD** |

Show Slide 7 to participants. Go through the points telling participants to think of a child in their caseload whom they think would benefit from direct work. Ask them to think what form this could take in terms of the framework we have been using.

SLIDE 7
Study child

- What direct work does this child need?
- How are you going to get started?
- Who else could help?
- What are you most worried about?
- Who is going to supervise you?
- Make a simple plan

Then ask participants to get into pairs and think which child on their caseload they are going to make their "study child" and start the direct work with. Say that, ideally, this should not be their most difficult case, so that they can gain confidence in selecting the technique they might use.

Tell participants to talk to each other for 10 minutes each about their study child. Remind participants that not all techniques have the same effect on each child.

Lead a group discussion with participants talking together about their choice of study child and their anxieties about this, and see if they have ideas to help each other.

Reassure participants by suggesting they start small (i.e. with a child under seven years old who needs some work but who is not too challenging, so that they can develop confidence). If there is no clinical supervision available through CAMHS or within their department, suggest that they look for the kind of peer support they have got whilst doing this course.

Other sources of support can come from the team around the child, from foster carers or family members, which can be really helpful because thinking with someone else can prompt a commonsensical approach.

20 minutes   **15**   **FINAL EXERCISE**

Ask participants to take out their handout showing the toy bag that was given to them in Session 1 and which they have been filling each session. Ask them to get into pairs to talk to each other for five minutes each about:

- one toy idea;
- one technique; or
- one thing that they have learnt as a result of being on the course or by being heard by a course member.

Suggest that they keep their own toy bags small so it all fits in a small rucksack under a desk.

Once the 10 minutes' thinking time is over, ask each participant to feed back their ideas to the rest of the group. During the final feedback, participants will probably enjoy having some refreshments to share.

Then ask them to suggest ideas on how they are going to keep themselves energised in this work – for example, is anyone available for clinical supervision in their office?

Remind participants that empathic listening is healing for children but that crisis work demands the ability to keep grounded and so it's essential that people working with children look after themselves so they are able to hear the child's voice. In order to be able to receive what the child needs to communicate, it is essential that you as the person listening to the child get enough breaks so you don't burn out and thereby become unable to hear the child.

To preserve a healthy worldview you need to be in touch with ordinary day-to-day living. Suggest that ways of keeping participants energised include taking short breaks as well as a two-week normal annual holiday. Also say that, if participants are going to do this kind of work, they need to make sure they do something creative to counterbalance it – to grow or make something.

10 minutes   **16**   **BRING COURSE TO A CLOSE**

Close the course by thanking course members for their participation and saying how much you, too, have enjoyed the journey with them.

It is helpful to acknowledge how emotionally draining this course can be. Also say that you hope they will be able to come to the follow-up session and bring some case material, whether positive or negative, as a result of what they have done and perhaps learned in these four sessions.

Hand out evaluation sheets, and allow five minutes for these to be completed.

SESSION 5
Follow-up session

OVERVIEW

	Section	Timing
1	Welcome and ball exercise	**10 minutes**
2	Goals for Session 5	**10 minutes**
3	Exercise: *Sharing work on the study child*	**40 minutes**
4	Feedback from groups	**45 minutes**
5	Break	**15 minutes**
6	Exercise: *Improving listening skills*	**1 hour**
7	*Rosebush exercise*	**30 minutes**
8	Lunch	**1 hour**
9	Afternoon activity: show DVD or introduce speaker	**1 hour**
10	Break	**15 minutes**
11	Games or techniques practice	**30 minutes**
12	Closing the course	**15 minutes**

PREPARATION

In advance of this session send out the date and programme to all participants. Remind them to bring some small part of their work done on their study child, either something written on paper or the object they used in this work so they can recall the event.

Reread Chapters 1, 4 and 5 of the *Handbook*.

PARTICULAR RESOURCES NEEDED FOR THIS SESSION

- You should have the *Handbook* available to consult during the day
- Ball for throwing
- Enough paper plates for each participant to have one, which will be covered with sand to make into a sandtray
- Some small toys or buttons for use on the sandtrays
- Coloured pens and paper or brushes, paints and paper
- A good selection of books to display from those mentioned during the first four sessions of this course
- *Jannie's Story*, a DVD available from Family Futures, which is about a child who re-enacts trauma in a new placement as a result of her past experiences
- Alternatively, another way to re-kindle participants' enthusiasm for direct work, especially if they have not done any yet, is to invite a speaker, like a psychotherapist or a drama, play or art therapist – someone who is prepared to give a short presentation and hold a question-and-answer session. This can really encourage continuing good practice so that "hearing the child's voice" becomes the norm
- Family circle game. A large piece of paper big enough for four people to stand on, and paint to colour it – see Handout 5.2
- Any other equipment you need for the techniques you have decided to practise

HANDOUTS

- 5.1: Session overview
- 5.2: Family building game

10 minutes

1 WELCOME AND BALL EXERCISE

Welcome participants. Remind them of the ground rules and rules on confidentiality.

Do the ball-playing exercise to relax participants and remind them of the names in the group. Ask participants to stand in a circle and throw the ball round to each other. As they do this, ask them to call out their own name.

SLIDE 1
Session 5: Follow up session

10 minutes

2 GOALS FOR SESSION 5

Show Slide 2, which gives the goals of the session.

SLIDE 2
Goals for Session 5

- Link theory to practice. To what extent has the course been integrated into your practice? What problems have you found in doing this work?
- What effect has this had on your agency's practice?
- Do you need more resources, more time or a different ethos? What can we do?
- To look at techniques and how they worked for you.
- Think about supporting parents with children who have difficulties.

40 minutes   **3**   **EXERCISE: SHARING WORK ON THE STUDY CHILD**

Ask participants to get into three groups and to tell each other about their experiences, using the tasks listed on the flipchart as follows:

- Recount what happened to their study child.
- Write down one thing the child said as a result of the work.
- What difficulties arose whilst doing the direct work?
- What departmental difficulties have you had?

45 minutes   **4**   **FEEDBACK FROM GROUPS**

Write up any reported difficulties. Decide if there is anything special you think participants need to go over again and be prepared to do another demonstration of any technique if necessary.

Use a workshop style to allow the group to air their difficulties and get the group to help each other through discussion.

Go through participants' practical difficulties in doing direct work and ask the group to think of ways to help with such difficulties. If they don't have any suggestions, you should provide ideas on how they might work with the children or ideas about how to change the department's ethos. For example, if they are finding that their department is not allowing space for children to be heard, you could suggest that participants who are having this problem do a small presentation of an idea or two from the course to teams in their department. This would be aimed at helping everyone to understand the importance of the work and how it will enable the department to make sure that "every child matters".

If you think this is a specific departmental problem you could put the participants working in that department or agency into a group together. Ask them to come up with solutions and say you will help them present these to their employers. For example, if children are moved into placement without preparation and the department disruption rate is very high, you could look at the department's assessment techniques. You could help the participant explain to their department why children who have had no life history work done before they go into permanency disrupt because of their behaviour, i.e. it may be because no one has helped them with their grief or to understand why they need new parents.

15 minutes   **5**   **BREAK**

1 hour   6   **EXERCISE: IMPROVING LISTENING SKILLS**

Ask participants to get into pairs with one of them taking on the role of "listener" and the other the social worker. Give them the sand trays made of small paper plates containing sand and toys or buttons. Ask them to share and describe, through play with the listener, one of their client's main issues. Ask them to take it in turns to do this.

While this is happening you should go round listening to the process taking place in each pair, gently changing the language if necessary (refer to the *Techniques* CD for a reminder about listening skills, or to Chapter 5 of the *Handbook*). Be sensitive when listening to participants, as they can feel challenged by such feedback. Use a very gentle approach such as 'I wonder if there might be another way to say or do that... '. Try to re-frame what they are saying so it is a bit less direct. For example, if you hear someone use a direct question like, 'Why did this happen?', etc. you could suggest that they might say instead 'I am wondering how this or that happened?'

30 minutes   7   **ROSEBUSH EXERCISE**

Introduce the rosebush exercise on identity, which you will find on the *Techniques CD* No. 68.

● Explain that the purpose of this exercise is to enhance the child's self-esteem.
● Give participants coloured pens, or paints, and paper.
● Spend 10 minutes on the exercise.
● Alternatively, depending on what your particular group's issues are, you could ask participants to get into pairs and make a drawing each of what they would like in their playroom or play area at the office or in the home.

After 10 minutes take feedback about the rosebush exercise. You could suggest questions like:

● Was the plant in a pot? If so, is it still thinking it's going to be moved to another garden?
● Is the plant settled in yet? How does the plant feel about being moved to this new garden?
● If there are no roots yet you could ask, 'I am wondering, how does the plant get food?'
● How long are the thorns (i.e. what might the child have to defend against)?

1 hour   8   **LUNCH**

1 hour   9   **AFTERNOON ACTIVITY**

Introduce either the DVD or a speaker, depending on how you have decided to run the afternoon.

Show DVD: Jannie's story

Explain that the reason for showing this DVD is that it relates to issues participants have looked at during the course, including negative internal working models and moving traumatised children into a new family. What this means is that after a "honeymoon period", the child might start acting out their negative working model as discussed in Session 1. This DVD shows powerfully how this can happen. This is something that workers really need to be aware of and have thought about in order to support families in which this happens.

After the film (which is 25 minutes long), invite feedback about it. Suggest to participants where they might find further help (see the *Handbook*, Chapter 3: *Neglect and trauma* under 'Managing difficult behaviour' and Chapter 4: *Grief and loss*, and on the *Techniques CD* under the same titles).

Discuss with participants any triggers that might be affecting the child.

Introduce speaker

For further details see the resources section at the start of this session.

15 minutes	10	**BREAK**

30 minutes **11 GAMES OR TECHNIQUES PRACTICE**

You could use the remaining time to play one of the two games ideas given below, which are intended to support parents and children in communicating feelings and understanding each other. These are suitable to use if you are training a group of social workers.

If you are training parents and carers, you could try out more of the attachment games listed in Chapter 2 of the *Handbook*.

Or, you might think it appropriate to spend the time practising more techniques, as this is valuable in enabling participants to gain sufficient confidence in running these activities themselves. For instance,

- the three island story (No. 70 on the *Techniques CD* and which involves clay and paint), or
- the loving and caring water game (No. 81 on the *Techniques CD*).

An alternative exercise is the family building game

The purpose of this game is to help the social worker end work with young people and their family and bring a new level of communication and cognition of how far they have all come and in building family bonds. For further details, refer participants to Handout 5.2, which describes how to set it up and role-play.

15 minutes **12 CLOSING THE COURSE**

End by reiterating some of the main points you have covered during this session and in the course as a whole.

Encourage participants to continue their direct work with children and remind them to ask for supervision. If possible, they should use a clinical supervisor if they are really stuck. Some departments have a clinical psychologist to assist everyone in the team occasionally in thinking about what is happening for a child. Generally it is helpful even if you are doing peer supervision to discuss the child and your work at least every third session for this type of direct work.

End by suggesting to participants that they perhaps form a small support group in their area. Express how much you have enjoyed working with them and say that you hope they will take all that they have learned into their future work.

References

Ainsworth M (1978) *Patterns of Attachment: A psychological study of the strange situation*, Hillsdale, JH: Lawrence Erlbaum Associates

Armstrong H, Britton B and Pickles T (1991) *Development Training Skills*, New York, NY: Longman Group Ltd

Axline V (1967) *Dibs, in Search of Self*, Harmondsworth: Penguin

Bowlby J (1969) *Attachment and Loss: Vol I, Attachment*, London: Hogarth Press

Bowlby J (1973) *Attachment and Loss: Vol II, Separation anxiety and anger*, London: Hogarth Press

Bowlby J (1988) *A Secure Base: Clinical applications of attachment theory*, London: Routledge

Briere J (1992) *Child Abuse Trauma: Theory and treatment of the lasting effects*, Newbury Park, CA: Sage Publications

Cairns K and Fursland E (2007) *Safer Caring: A training programme*, London: BAAF

Cole B (1995) *Mummy Laid an Egg*, London: Red Fox

Cole M and Cole SR (1996) *The Development of Children* (third edition), New York, NY: WH Freeman

Corrigan M and Floud C (1990) 'A framework for direct work with children in care', Practice brief, *Adoption & Fostering*, 14:2, pp 28–32

Delaney R (1991) *Fostering Changes*, Fort Collins: WJC

Department for Education and Skills (2003) *Every Child Matters*, London: DfES

Department of Health (2000) *Framework for the Assessment of Children in Need and their Families*, London: Department of Health

Falhberg V (1994) *A Child's Journey through Placement*, London: BAAF

Fleet, R (1994) 'Filial therapy for adoptive children and parents', in O' Connor KJ and Schaefer CE (eds), *Handbook of Play Therapy, Volume II, Advances and innovations*, New York, NY: John Wiley & Sons, pp 371–385)

Gerhardt S (2004) *Why Love Matters: How love shapes the baby's brain*, Hove: Brunner Routledge

Howarth J and Morrison T (1999) *Effective Staff Training in Social Care: From theory to practice*, Basingstoke: Routledge & Young Ltd

Hughes D (2000) *Facilitating Developmental Attachment: The road to emotional recovery and behavioural change in foster and adopted children*, New York, NY: Jason Aronson Inc Publishers

Jewett C (1984) *Separation and Loss*, London: Batsford

Kubler-Ross E (1969) *On Death and Dying*, London: Tavistock Publications

Main M and Hesse E (1990) 'Parent unresolved traumatic experiences are related to infant disorganised attachment status: is frightened or frightening parental behaviour the linking mechanism?', in Greenberg M, Cicchetti D and Cummings E (eds) *Attachment in the Preschool Years: Theory, research and intervention*, Chicago, IL: University of Chicago Press, pp. 126–139

Marvin R, Cooper G, Hoffman K and Powell B (2002) 'The Circle of Security Project: attachment based intervention with caregiver-pre-school child dyads', *Attachment and Human Development*, 4:1, pp 107–124

Pallett C, Blackeby K, Yule W, Weissman R and Scott S with Fursland E (2007) *Managing Difficult Behaviour: A handbook for foster carers of the under 12s*, London: BAAF

Perry B and Pollard R (1997) 'Altered brain development following global neglect in early childhood', paper presented at Society for Neuroscience annual meeting

Perry B and Pollard R (1998) 'Homeostasis, stress, trauma and adaptation: a neurodevelopmental view of childhood trauma', *Child and Adolescent Psychiatric Clinics of North America*, 7:1, pp 22–46

Prior V and Glaser D (2006) *Understanding Attachment and Attachment Disorders: Theory, evidence and practice*, London: Jessica Kingsley Publishers

Rees J (2009) *Life Story Books for Adopted Children*, London: Jessica Kingsley Publishers

Rogers C (1961) *On Becoming a Person: A therapist's view of psychotherapy*, London: Bowden

Sunderland M (1998) *Draw on your Emotions*, Oxon: Winslow Press

Stern D (1985) *The Interpersonal World of the Infant*, New York, NY: Basic Books

Van der Kolk B, McFarlane A and Weisaeth L (eds) (1996) *Traumatic Stress: The effects of overwhelming experience on mind, body and society*, New York, NY: The Guilford Press

Van Fleet, R (1994) *Filial Therapy: Strengthening parent-child relationships through play*, Sarasota, FL: Professional Resource Press

Van Fleet R and Topham G (2011) 'Filial therapy for maltreated and neglected children', in Drewes AA, Bratton SC and Schaefer CE, *Integrative Play Therapy*, New York, NY: John Wiley & Sons, pp 153–176

Woldt AL and Toman SM (eds) (2005) *Gestalt Therapy: History, theory and practice*, Thousand Oaks, CA: Sage Publications